Also by the Author

Winds of Change: Korean Women in America (Nonfiction)

Sylvia's Garden (Fiction)

THOUSAND LUCKS

A War Survival Story of a
Thirteen-Year-Old Girl

Diana Yu

Copyright © 2023 Diana Yu.

All rights reserved. No part of this book may be used or reproduced by any means, graphic, electronic, or mechanical, including photocopying, recording, taping or by any information storage retrieval system without the written permission of the author except in the case of brief quotations embodied in critical articles and reviews.

This book is a work of non-fiction. Unless otherwise noted, the author and the publisher make no explicit guarantees as to the accuracy of the information contained in this book and in some cases, names of people and places have been altered to protect their privacy.

Archway Publishing books may be ordered through booksellers or by contacting:

Archway Publishing
1663 Liberty Drive
Bloomington, IN 47403
www.archwaypublishing.com
844-669-3957

Because of the dynamic nature of the Internet, any web addresses or links contained in this book may have changed since publication and may no longer be valid. The views expressed in this work are solely those of the author and do not necessarily reflect the views of the publisher, and the publisher hereby disclaims any responsibility for them.

Any people depicted in stock imagery provided by Getty Images are models, and such images are being used for illustrative purposes only. Certain stock imagery © Getty Images.

ISBN: 978-1-6657-4681-6 (sc)
ISBN: 978-1-6657-4679-3 (hc)
ISBN: 978-1-6657-4680-9 (e)

Library of Congress Control Number: 2023913131

Print information available on the last page.

Archway Publishing rev. date: 09/19/2023

I dedicate this book to my mother, Kim Hyun Shin, and my husband, Tom Tull, whose love enabled me to write *Thousand Lucks*.

Acknowledgements

I acknowledge the following with sincere gratitude:

For manuscript reviews:
Valerie Mylowe
Betty Fung
Cindy Buckner
Karen Leigh Gray
Judith Anne Gray
Gwenn Baldwin
Summer Wood

Adam Weisman, for his technical expertise. Adam was always available when I needed his help.

1

That Day

"Hurry!" Kitchen *Halmuhni* (Grandmother) said to struggling Yu Hyun Jung. "You are getting your white blouse all dirty. Look at the smudges from the charcoal."

As usual, Yu Hyun Jung was late for school. It seemed to take her longer and longer each morning to get ready. All the other girls were already at the daily morning drill down at the track field.

It was June 25, 1950, seemingly a normal summer day in the capital city of Seoul; the balmy blue sky had not even a hint of cloud. Snugly settled in the West Gate section of the city, Ewha Girls' Middle School was a peaceful enclave for girls from refined Korean families. But even after one whole year at the school, the thirteen-year-old Yu Hyun Jung was still having a hard time getting adjusted. She struggled to fit in with the more citified and sophisticated girls.

Her parents, especially her father, had insisted that she attended Ewha, founded by an American Methodist missionary, Mrs. Mary Scranton, in 1886. Hyun Jung had to take a three-day entrance exam to get into Ewha, the top-tier girls-only school in the country. In 1949, only three hundred twenty girls got accepted out of over nine hundred applicants.

Hyun Jung's family cared a lot about how she grew up in this Confucian-based society, properly, for her class. In fact, before coming to Ewha, when she lived at her province home, Jin San, Hyun Jung wasn't allowed to interact with just any girls in the village. Sometimes, even girls from her own extended family, with the same surname, were off-limits for her.

Her grandfather, Yu Kyung Duck Gong, was vigilant regarding which girls his only granddaughter associated with. One time, when Hyun Jung came home after talking to a girl near her house, he confronted her.

"Yes, sir," she answered, softly.

"The girl you just chatted with, her grandmother was a concubine," he told her with a low, hushed voice. Hyun Jung listened without interrupting the grandfather. He continued, "You are not to engage in a conversation with a girl brought up in such a household."

Hyun Jung knew who her grandfather was speaking about, the girl's grandmother. She had heard the village grownups talking about the lady before.

Hyun Jung always obeyed her grandfather. She never doubted his good intentions for her. She believed that whatever her grandfather told her to do was for her own good. She, in fact, appreciated her grandfather paying so much attention to her, when her own father was away from home so much. Her father couldn't come home, because the Japanese would arrest him for his anti-Japanese occupation activities.

Her father, Yu Chin San, thought a lot about Hyun Jung, even though his political activities kept him away from home most of the time. He thought a lot about his only daughter. If she stayed in Jin San, he feared she might not know how to relate to girls from certain families when she grew up. This was the main reason he and his father agreed to send her to Ewha in Seoul, so she could learn how to interact with city girls from Seoul.

Now that World War II was over, the Japanese occupiers fled the country, and Hyun Jung's father could come back to their Seoul home. However, she had to live on campus. Her father insisted that commuting to class each day wasn't the right or best choice, although most girls commuted. Out of twenty-one hundred girls at the Ewha Girls' Middle School, only sixty lived in the campus dorm.

All the girls who lived on campus, except Hyun Jung, were from provinces. Her family had a home in Seoul as well, but her father was afraid of the busy traffic in the city.

Whenever she asked why she had to live on campus and not at home, he would say, "A machine can always breakdown. A car is a machine."

She understood that what he really wanted was for her to learn to interact with other girls and grow up to be a lady. He wanted her to be modern, yet proper for a girl from a *yangban* family. She sensed that her parents felt she would not get the right training or make the right associations if she lived at home and associated only with the girls from their neighborhood. On the other hand, living on campus would give her more opportunity to learn to interact with a better class of girls.

Living at the dorm may have served the wishes of the grownups; however, the young girl was not happy about the situation she found herself in. She preferred to live at home, with many conveniences and the pampering from her mother and helpers. Hyun Jung had specific complaints about dorm life. The thing she liked the least was taking a communal bath, where others could see her naked body.

"How can you wash yourself if you don't take your clothes off?" the housemother, Oh, often asked Hyun Jung in a scolding tone.

Hyun Jung wouldn't say anything. Instead, she'd quickly pick up a bucket, unbutton her sleepwear top, and pour water from the bucket onto herself.

One Saturday evening, she looked around the large communal bath hall and slowly began to take her top off.

Just then, she heard, "Hurry, take off your top so you can wash yourself well."

It was Oh's piercing, loud voice. She first adjusted her brown rimmed glasses and shouted at Hyun Jung from the entranceway of the bath hall. Hyun Jung's eyes, more closely than usual, noted the blue and white tiles in the bath hall.

In addition to the communal bath, Hyun Jung disliked eating meals with six other girls and having to eat fast. This confused her, because at home she was told to eat slowly, swallow only after chewing forty times, for example.

In addition, Hyun Jung disliked having to wipe the dining table after each meal. She had to do this with a smelly wet rag. Still, the worst thing for her was pressing her own school uniform. If Hyun Jung had to choose what she liked least about her dorm life, she would probably say everything.

On this morning, June 25, 1950, Hyun Jung struggled to press her school uniform, a long-sleeved white blouse, with the wooden-handled charcoal-burning iron. The grandmother shook her head and moved close to Hyun Jung, saying, "Here, let me help." She then continued, "You'll be late again. Go, get yourself ready for school, hear?"

"Thank you, Halmuhni," Hyun Jung said and rushed to get ready to report to the morning drill held at the school track field below.

"If you were living at home like the day girls, I am sure you wouldn't have to worry about ironing your own school uniform."

Everything about dorm life was simply miserable for Yu Hyun Jung. The only person who understood her and often came to her rescue was the kindly Kitchen Halmuhni. In fact, she was so helpful to all the girls and never told on anyone to the housemother. Hyun Jung loved every wrinkle on Kitchen Halmuhni's broad, square face. Contrary to Oh, Halmuhni was sympathetic to all the sixty girls who lived at the hilltop dorm; everyone there loved her.

"Late again." Hyun Jung heard Oh's icy voice as she trudged down the hill. She didn't have to look to see whose voice it was; she knew.

Thinking of the housemother's parchment-tight face, Hyun Jung picked up her steps and rushed down to the track field below. She prepared to join the other girls, who normally were lined up in straight rows, like chopsticks.

On that day, June 25, 1950, however, as Hyun Jung came to an edge of the hill and looked down to the field, she noticed the girls were spread out in confusion. Hyun Jung rushed down the meandering, lilac-scented path toward the track field. As soon as she arrived, all the girls were rushing toward the school gate. Not knowing what else to do, Hyun Jung joined them as they ran like a herd of goats.

"What's happening?" she asked Eun Ja, who was running right next to her.

Eun Ja replied, "The Communists from the North, came over the 38th Parallel; they invaded Seoul last night."

The girls ran frantically toward the school gate.

As she got closer to the gate, Hyun Jung heard family members calling out the other girls' names: Soon Ja ya, Ji Sook ah, Jung Oak ah. Hyun Jung listened anxiously for her own name to be called but didn't hear it. *Something terrible must have happened to my family,* she thought with a heavy heart.

The other girls pushed Hyun Jung aside and ran to the old gray tile-roofed front gate of the school.

Still, she heard everyone's name but her own.

She stretched her neck, checking to see if anyone had come for her, but didn't recognize anyone. *No one came for me,* she thought, and felt humiliated to let the other girls find out that no one in her family cared enough to come for her.

Only a few minutes passed since the girls began running toward the gate, but most of the day girls were picked up. They were swept away, gone, like the receding ocean tide. The schoolyard turned into an instant ghost town. Just a few girls were left. The only ones left were the girls from provinces who lived in the dorm, up on the hill.

Feeling neglected and confused, Hyun Jung dragged her feet back up the hill, to her old redbrick, two-story dorm building. She remembered just one year before, how she had been dropped off by her older brother, Joong Yul, and how heavy her steps had been to enter the front door of the residence hall. Today, with all the commotion earlier, she felt alone and wanted to be away from the school and be with her family.

"Came"

Hyun Jung finally made it to her room on the second floor at her dorm. She was glad to see Eun Ja again and asked, "You still here?"

"*Ueng,*" Eun Ja answered and disappeared into her room, two doors away. These two girls were the same age and got along well. Still, Hyun Jung was reluctant to tell her friend how rejected she felt by her family. Without saying a word to anyone, Hyung Jung slowly stepped into her empty dorm room.

A minute later, Eun Ja came into Hyun Jung's room and said, "They want us to come down to the gym; bring your beddings with you."

"*Ung*" [Got it], Hyun Jung mumbled with a nod.

"But why are you still here, instead of going home?" Eun Ja asked. "You have a home in Seoul."

"So what?" Hyun Jung continued, "No one came for me. Everybody in my family is still down in Jin San; the election, you know."

"Oh, I know," Eun Ja said, lowering her voice. "It's too bad your father didn't win."

Hyun Jung appreciated Eun Ja's sympathy. Eun Ja was a head shorter than Hyun Jung and was bouncier and more cheerful. Eun Ja also had adjusted better to her dorm life than Hyun Jung had, so far.

"They want us to be at the gym right now," she said.

Hugging her thick, rolled-up mat and comforter with her right arm, and holding on to the sunbaked brown metal rail of the tennis court below on the left, Hyun Jung cautiously followed Eun Ja down the meandering narrow path to the basement gym.

When they entered the gym, Hyun Jung noticed the youthful-looking gym teacher, Mr. Chang, standing by the entranceway, checking the girls in. "Twenty-five," he counted. "I think that's all." Mr. Chang was talking to Mr. Pyo, the vice principal of the school.

It was dark gray inside of the basement gym. The only light came from the three half-windows on the north side of room.

The girls were directed to place their beddings up against the north side of the wall, directly under the row of short windows on the north side of the room. Mr. Chang and Mr. Pyo positioned the girls there to avoid the possibility of the girls getting hit by stray bullets that might fly through the windows.

As soon as the girls settled themselves down with their beddings, Mr. Chang, the gym teacher, told them to come to the front of the room. When all the girls got to the front of the gym room, he began a safety demonstration.

"You all have to know what to do when the bombs drop down with a thundering sound," he said, standing in front of the girls. He continued, "The sound could be so loud it tears up your eardrums."

Since the Communist invasion of Seoul the night before, of the sixty girls who had been living at the dorm, only twenty-five were left. Many of these girls had come from provinces. For some, the Communist North may not yet have invaded their southern hometowns; however, the guerrilla havoc all over the country prevented them from going home.

"Watch me, watch my hands," the gym teacher said, as he used both thumbs to plug his ears. "Now, you do this with your thumbs and cover your eyes, like this."

No one spoke, but each person followed the teacher, step by step, diligently.

Mr. Chang continued, "Then, just drop yourself down on the ground, flat, wherever you are, like this." He gave a demonstration. When Mr. Chang finished showing them what to do in an emergency situation, the girls repeated what he did in front of them.

"All of you are very good at following Mr. Chang," Mr. Pyo said. "Now, do it for me, this time. I want to make sure you are all familiar with what to do when the bombs drop."

The girls repeated the demonstration for Mr. Pyo as diligently as they had done for Mr. Chang.

Hyun Jung spent the whole night alternating between dozing and listening to the sound of cannon and gunshots. All the other girls appeared to have fallen asleep. For Hyun Jung Yu, however, the occasional whisperings amongst the teachers kept her awake.

The gym was still dark gray. Hyun Jung held her breath and heard, "Came."

No one responded, but the same man continued, "They took Seoul, early this morning."

She recognized the voice. It was Principal Jo, the school's principal.

3

Walking In Dead City

Back in the dorm, the girls were told to move down to the first floor. Hyun Jung's new room on the first floor was smaller and narrower than the room she had been used to ever since she first had enrolled at Ewha. It was up on the second floor. The new room, on the first floor, had only one small brown metal-framed bed, shoved up against the left side of the wall. Besides the bed, the room had no other furniture, not even a chair to sit on. The only thing Hyun Jung liked about the new room on the first floor was a big window facing the courtyard on the north side. She liked to look through the window at a large lilac bush with purple flowers.

It had been only one day since the Communists invaded Seoul, but to Hyun Jung, it seemed like years. Although no one told her, she knew, from her heart, that her own family was in big danger because of the large numbers of Communist guerillas in the nearby mountains around Jin San, her hometown. Mount Ji Ri and the smaller mountains closer to Geum San, the county seat, were well known for Communist guerillas raising frequent havoc, irritating the villagers.

The morning of the second day in her new dorm room, Hyun Jung took out a small suitcase from under the bed, then took out a large piece of pink silk cloth with floral patterns and spread it open on the bed. In the center of the cloth, she placed her favorite peach-colored nylon dress. Her mother had bought the American dress for her just last year, and she had not yet worn it. She had been saving it for a special occasion. After the dress, she placed a pair of high-top brown leather shoes she had also been saving for a special occasion. Finally, she put a framed picture of her father and the president of the country, Rhee Seung Mahn, along with some other men. After arranging these things on the center of the square piece of cloth, she tied the four corners of the cloth and made it into a small carrying bag. She had decided to walk home.

Hyun Jung thought about telling Ko Yung Hee, her *Kyo Je Unee* (fellowship big sister), who was in twelfth grade at Ewha and lived in the same dorm, but decided not to.

Her thought was, *My family didn't care to come and get me. Why should anybody else care whether I live or die?* She felt sorry for her situation.

In her mind, Hyun Jung knew her family wouldn't be at their Seoul house in Choong Shin Dong, the East Gate section of Seoul. Still, she needed to go and see it for herself. Besides, there was nothing to do in the Ewha campus, which had suddenly turned lifeless. She harbored a hope that somebody might be at her house, even hiding quietly in the attic, or someplace.

Wearing her school uniform with its white long-sleeved cotton blouse and knee-length navy-blue skirt, Hyun Jung began her walk to her home in the East Gate neighborhood. It was located on the exact opposite part of Seoul as the Ewha campus was located on the West Gate section of the capital city. She would have to walk clear across the big city. She knew that it would take a chunk of the day. However, she decided to go ahead with her plan. She was prepared for disappointments if she found out no one was at the house, and even dangerous if confronted by Communist soldiers.

Just as Hyun Jung was about to leave the dorm building, she ran into Eun Ja. "Going somewhere?"

"Home."

"Did you tell the housemother?"

"No," Hyun Jung said. "She won't care."

"Will you walk all the way?"

"What choice do I have?" Hyun Jung asked, looking straight at Eun Ja. "Either that, or I stay around here and get killed."

"Okay, if you must," Eun Ja said, looking worried. "Then, hurry. Get going; it's a long way to your house in the East Gate neighborhood, all the way from the west to the east section of Seoul."

With both hands tightly hugging the small pink bag against her bosom, Hyun Jung began the journey to her home located in the East Gate neighborhood.

Since the first day the Communists marched into Seoul, everything in Yu Hyun Jung's life had changed. The only thing that remained constant in her life was the balmy, beautiful cobalt-blue sky and the beautiful lilac-scented Ewha campus. The sky didn't even have one smudge of cloud; another perfect June day.

Sounds and Sights of Dead City

Hyun Jung was alarmed to find Ewha's main gate wide open, because she had known the heavy tile-roofed gate was always kept locked after school hours. The Watchman Grandfather was nowhere to be seen.

Once outside of the school gate, Hyun Jung quietly checked around by looking left and right more than once. She took a deep breath before beginning her journey across Seoul, the big capital city. She will have to walk from the West Gate across the whole city to the East Gate neighborhood. Hyun Jung noticed there was not even the slightest sound or movement immediately outside of the campus. Soon she walked past the gray-stoned American-style house where Miss Martin, one of the two American English conversation teachers at Ewha, lived.

Hyun Jung passed Jung Dong Methodist Church on the right. It had been her church since she first came to Ewha. Afterwards, she made a left turn toward the smooth wide hill to reach Jong Ro Boulevard, the main east-west road of the city. She didn't see or hear any signs of humanity - - only her own quiet, insecure footsteps.

She made a gentle left turn onto a wide, well-kept road, when, suddenly, to her surprise, she spotted two Communist soldiers. They sat quietly with their backs against the gray stone wall of Duck Soo Palace. It was the very first time Hyun Jung had seen Communist soldiers. Their uniforms looked different from the one her brother, Joong Yul, wore in the South Korean army. The uniforms of the Communist soldiers were a yellowish, faded mustard green. Their helmets were covered with actual tree branches, with leaves still attached to them.

She was about ten feet from them. Hyun Jung quickly lowered her eyes, trying to act like she didn't see them. No one spoke. She kept up with her steps while still trying to appear unalarmed. Her heart raced. She kept her eyes lowered. Through the corner of her eyes, she caught a glance of one of the soldiers. He was looking her way while the other one was busy fiddling with his rifle. The scene of the two soldiers gave Hyun Jung the impression that nothing special happened. She kept up with her walking.

They looked young, not more than seventeen or eighteen. But at one point, she noticed they both turned and looked toward her. She quickly turned her head back to its original position and kept walking as if she didn't see anything. They appeared to be ignoring her. She breathed a quiet sigh of relief.

There was no sign of life near the capital city's Supreme Court. Hyun Jung passed abandoned American-style buildings with stone walls and gray rooftop tiles. After passing Kyung Ki Girls' Middle School on her left, she kept walking toward the center of Seoul's once-bustling road, Jong Ro Boulevard.

After passing numerous abandoned shops and office buildings, Hyun Jung finally reached Jong Ro Boulevard, the main road between the East Gate and the West Gate of the city.

She noticed several streetcars, but none of them moved. They had just stopped on their tracks. Nothing appeared to be moving in this city of nine million people. Hyun Jung was mindful of how lifeless the whole place was. Like her school, the street was empty and quiet—suffocatingly quiet, like a vast desert.

Other than the streetcars, there were no other vehicles in sight. All the shops were closed, shut. She saw no sign of humanity anywhere. With her head still down, Hyun Jung continued her steps forward. Her home in the East Gate neighborhood was still a long way away.

5

"Nobody's Here"

Hyun Jung finally made it to her house in Choong Shin Dong, in the East Gate section of Seoul. She quietly looked around and then cautiously peered near and far. Then she pushed the heavy front gate open. She didn't see anyone or hear any sound. She stepped into the foyer and paused instead of going right into the main part of the house. It was eerily quiet, as if it had turned into a strange place, instead of being her own home.

Then, suddenly, a booming male voice made her take a quick step back. "Nobody's here." Hyun Jung looked up and saw a Communist soldier with a rifle pointing directly at her. "All left … gone."

She quickly turned her head to face the soldier, who had badges on his shoulder pad and helmet. The badges were of the North Korean flags of red star with blue and white colors. In addition, she saw a picture of Kim Il Sung, the founder of the Communist country, the Democratic People's Republic of Korea. Hyun Jung quickly lowered her head and then, without saying a word, timidly back-stepped out of her house.

She knew her mother was still in Jin San, cleaning up after the campaign where her father had been defeated for the National Parliament by a woman candidate, Tae Jung Shin, on May 10, one month and ten days ago, to be exact. Hyun Jung's father, Yu Chin San, had run as an independent for a seat at the National

Parliament of South Korea, also known as the Republic of Korea. His opponent had a wide name recognition in the country. She was the only woman cabinet member of the Rhee Seung Mahn administration. More specifically, she was the first female cabinet member in the Republic of Korea's history. She was the Minister of Commerce in the patriarchal society. Her American university education distinguished her. Also, none other than the president of the country, Dr. Rhee Seung Mahn's generous contribution to her campaign helped her succeed.

Being chased out of her own house, with no place else to go, Hyun Jung decided to visit her neighbor across the street. She tiptoed across the narrow walkway that led to the neighbor's house. She had visited the house once before with her mother and remembered sharing a noodle lunch with the gray-haired Halmuhni.

When she arrived at the neighbor's house, she looked around quietly and then knocked on the wooden gate. To her surprise, the gray-haired Halmuhni timidly opened the gate and stepped aside to let Hyun Jung in. Together, without saying a word to each other, they walked into the wood-paneled dining room, with Western-style dining table and chairs. They still didn't say a word to each other. Halmuhni looked more scared than surprised.

"Everyone left," she whispered.

"I know," Hyun Jung answered.

"You knew?"

Hyun Jung nodded. "I was just there."

The Halmuhni was alone in her house. The younger ones ran away, but she decided to stay, thinking the Communists wouldn't harm this gray-haired old woman. Besides, her old body wouldn't be much for walking, even if she had joined her younger family members on their southward escape.

"So what are you going to do?" Halmuhni asked, looking worried. "Where are you staying?"

"Go back to my dorm at school, ma'am."

"Poor thing," Halmuhni said, wiping tears on her sleeve. "Be careful, always. You will be all right. Your mother was a kind person. You will be rewarded for her kind deeds." Slowly, nodding her head, Halmuhni continued, "I am certain of that."

After sharing a bowl of noodles with the Halmuhni at her old neighborhood in Choong Shin Dong, Hyun Jung headed back toward the West Gate neighborhood, to the Ewha campus. Her school dorm was the only place she knew she could still go to in this world that had turned upside down for her since just yesterday.

It was a long walk back to the dorm on the West Gate. Once-bustling Jong Ro Boulevard was still empty and lifeless. There was no sign of humanity anywhere. Hyun Jung kept placing one foot before the other, toward her school dorm, rushing her steps as if someone was chasing her. The streets in Seoul couldn't be quieter or more lifeless. She didn't see anyone, only the empty shops and the streetcars that were stopped on the track. She retraced her steps, with the Kyung Ki Girls' Middle School and Duck Soo Palace on the right.

Hyun Jung briefly remembered how unhappy she'd been that day, just a little bit over one year before, when her brother Joong Yul had dropped her off at the redbrick school dorm. Now, however, she was grateful the dorm was there. She still had a place to go.

After walking for hours, Hyun Jung finally arrived back at the open gate at the campus of the Ewha Girls' Middle School.

At the dorm, she went directly to her room and dropped on the bed to rest her tired feet. She dozed.

Eun Ja stopped by and woke Hyun Jung up. She whispered, "Most of the girls have already gone. Only sixteen left." She continued, "You must be tired."

All in all, the two girls looked happy to see each other.

"I walked all the way to the East Gate and back," Hyun Jung said, whining, "Oh, my feet!"

"Let me make you feel a little better," Eun Ja said and began massaging Hyun Jung's feet.

"The whole city of Seoul is like a cemetery," Hyun Jung said, shaking her head. "Everything's dead."

"Really?" Eun Ja was impressed that her girlfriend had actually walked so far and come back safely. "How was it?" Eun Ja asked in a hushed tone of voice. "What did you see?"

"I didn't see one person on Jong Ro Boulevard," Hyun Jung said. "The streetcars all have stopped. I didn't see any of them moving. Jong Ro is deserted."

"Everybody either took off or is hiding, I guess," Eun Ja whispered.

"How about you?" Hyun Jung asked. "Not going home?"

Eun Ja shrugged and said, "I don't expect anyone to come for me." She continued, "The guerillas from Ji Ri Mountain, you know, already took my village. I'm sure of that."

"That reminds me of something," Hyun Jung said.

"What's that?"

"My brother, Joong Yul, is supposed to be fighting the Communists in the foothills of Ji Ri Mountain," Hyun Jung said. "They say the Communists from the North have built tunnels from Pyung Yang, North Korea's capital, all the way down to the southernmost end, Ji Ri Mountain!"

"Really?"

"Yeah, it's not far from Jin San, my hometown, you know."

"Don't worry too much," Eun Ja said. "Your family was kind to the villagers; that goes far."

6

Looting

Eun Ja sat in Hyun Jung's first-floor dorm room and whined, "There's nothing to do." Then, she slowly went over and pulled up the heavy wood-framed window.

"No housemother to scold us," Hyun Jung said, jokingly. "I like that we have nothing to do." Eun Ja was her only friend in this suddenly eerily quiet girls' school campus.

Hyun Jung and Eun Ja were both in the eighth grade and were the youngest in the dorm. Since everyone else was older, these two stuck together. In Korea's Confucian hierarchical custom, it was expected that the two girls would associate with one another because they were the same age; they didn't have to be deferential to each other. Girls the same age could use informal *bahn mal* (half words) when they talked. They were equal and didn't have to use honorifics to each other. They could relax and just enjoy being with each other.

Hyun Jung said, teasingly, "So you miss that time we all got in trouble with the Home Economics teacher, Miss Kwon, for not cleaning up the classroom like she wanted us to do?"

"Yeah," Eun Ja said. "She was too much."

"Remember her going around with her white gloves on?" Hyun Jung said, shaking her head left to right. "And checking out the entire windowsills to see if we got all the dirt cleaned?"

"I still miss it," Eun Ja said, then she added, "Let's go to see our classroom."

"Let's," Eun Ja repeated, looking at Hyun Jung's eyes. "Let's."

Holding on to the warm metal rail of the tennis court on the left, and inhaling the sweet smell of the lilac blossoms, Hyun Jung followed Eun Ja down the hill towards the classroom. They were glad the double doors to the Moo Goong Wha Hall were left unlocked. The two girls rushed up to their empty second-floor classroom. As expected, Eun Ja beat Hyun Jung to it.

In their empty classroom, the two girls saw the row of wooden desks and chairs lined up like dried-up firewood.

"So quiet," Eun Ja said, turning toward her friend. Hyun Jung, without saying a word, followed Eun Ja into the classroom.

"What did you expect?" Hyun Jung whispered, forcefully. "Nothing's the same anymore."

Eun Ja rushed over to the back of the room, toward the row of large wall-to-wall glass windows. She looked out on the neighborhood below. Just two days before, it had been a bustling neighborhood with gray stone Western-style buildings.

"Look, look," Eun Ja whispered urgently. "Come here, hurry." She motioned with her hand while her eyes looked out at the American teacher's home. "Look, the teacher's house is being looted. Hurry… Hurry!"

"Oh, no," Hyun Jung lamented. "It's Miss Martin's house. They are stealing everything. See those white papers they are dropping all over the ground?"

"Yeah," Eun Ja said. "What are they?"

"You put them on your lap when you eat," Hyun Jung said, keeping her eyes still on the ground of Miss Martin's gray-stone American-style house. "They are called *napukins*."

"What?" Eun Ja asked. "What are they?"

"Napukins."

"How do you know that?"

"I was at Miss Martin's house last Christmas Eve."

"Really?" Eun Ja asked. "How come I wasn't there?"

"Well, I don't know," Hyun Jung said, shaking her head. "Miss Martin invited three girls from our dorm. Our house mother, Miss Oh, asked me to go with her."

Hyun Jung remembered how she and Miss Oh and two upper classmen, Jung Joo Sill and Ko Yung Hee, walked from the dorm, down through the main part of the school ground, unlocked the gate, and crossed Jung Dong Road, then entered the large yard of Miss Martin's house.

Hyun Jung still remembered that night clearly, as if it happened just yesterday:

It was a dark and cold December night, just last year, 1949. Miss Oh walked over there with two upper class girls, Joo Sill and Yung Hee; Hyun Jung was the only eighth grader, the youngest one in the group. The seventh graders didn't count in selecting the special small group to visit the American teacher's home on that Christmas Eve.

That night, they had stepped into a different world. The very first thing that caught Hyun Jung's eye was the pretty tree at the right side of the entranceway in Miss Martin's American-style home.

It was the very first time Hyun Jung had seen an ordinary tree, like a pine tree, so beautifully decorated with red, yellow, green, and blue lights. Pine trees were very common in Korea. But she had never before realized they could be decorated so beautifully. Other than the tree, the entrance of the house was dark, something between the color of burnt umber and dark gray. Hyun Jung had thought, Americans know how to make even a common pine tree look so beautiful.

Growing up in Jin San, the small mountainous farming village, she had been familiar with pine trees. They were the most common trees around, but it never crossed her mind that they could be decorated pretty this way. Hyun Jung thought, *Americans are special people. They know how to make everything beautiful! They can even* make a common thing like a pine tree into such a special beauty! No wonder the name of the country is Mi Gook, Beautiful Nation."

"I fell in love with America then and have been ever since," Hyun Jung said to Eun Ja.

Hyun Jung continued telling Eun Ja how Miss Martin had greeted her group that night. With her signature wide smile, she showed a deep dimple on her right cheek. She led them into the inner part of the house, and in the living room, the teacher gave each girl a white paper napkin to place on their lap.

Then, Miss Martin passed around a plate of pretty red and green cookies and candies. The girls used the white napkins when they ate those candies and round cookies. Hyun Jung still remembered how impressed she was that night.

"I wonder where they are now," Eun Ja asked.

"Who?"

"Miss Martin and Mrs. Sours."

"They flew away, by airplane, I'm sure," Hyun Jung said.

"They were lucky to just fly away when danger broke out," Eun Ja said. "I wish I could do that, just fly away. Fly away from all the troubles of this world."

"Have you been on a plane?" Hyun Jung asked.

"Me?" Eun Ja replied. "No, never. Haven't even seen one."

From their classroom window, the two girls, holding their breath, quietly watched people carrying out the boxes and boxes of goods on their shoulders and dropping things like napkins and canned goods.

Ewha Girls' Middle School had two American teachers: Miss Martin and Mrs. Sours. Miss Martin was the younger of the two. She was no more than nineteen or twenty years old. She had a mop of curly reddish blonde hair, with a face round like a full moon. She taught English conversation to the eighth graders on Mondays.

Mrs. Sours was the other American teacher. She taught English conversation on Thursdays. Miss Martin was more popular among the students. All of them wanted to be in Miss Martin's class because she was younger and smiled a lot. Mrs. Sours, on the other hand, was almost fifty and had a boney, triangular-shaped face with a pointed chin. She wore glasses, and the wrinkles on her forehead seemed deeper when she scolded the students. Her cold chartreuse-green eyes seemed to see through your head and knew what you were thinking. She also could see all the kids in her class at one glance. She seemed to have eyes in the back of her head. The girls in her class knew they couldn't get away with anything.

Unfortunately, Hyun Jung had Mrs. Sours for her Thursday English conversation class. Because she wasn't in Miss Martin's class, the Christmas party invitation was especially memorable. It had opened the eyes and mind of the thirteen-year-old little girl from the mountainous farming village of Jin San in South Choong Chung Do, south of Seoul and Daejeon.

On the way back to the dorm, Eun Ja stepped closer and whispered, "Did you know that the rice store on West Gate Market is now closed?"

"Really?" Hyun Jung said. "So then how can we live?"

"Yeah, no more rice for us."

The rice merchants, like everyone else in Seoul, closed their shops and ran for their lives. All headed south, away from the Communist invaders. Those who didn't take off were hiding behind locked doors and holding their breath. They were fearful of being reported by someone and persecuted for being "capitalist merchant pigs."

7

"No More Rice"

Ko Yung Hee was interested in having Yu Hyun Jung as her younger sister. When Hyun Jung first entered Ewha Girls' Middle School, Ko Yung Hee, who was eighteen years old then and in eleventh grade, had approached Yu Hyun Jung through an intermediary. It was a rather common practice for girls in Korean schools to have a *kyoje unnee* (fellowship older sister) and a *kyoje dongseng* (fellowship younger sibling).

Yung Hee was the youngest of six children in her family and had no younger sister. In Hyun Jung's case, she was the only daughter and wanted an older sister. Through Jung Joo Sill, another eleventh grader, Yung Hee had asked Hyun Jung to be her younger sister. The asking was always carried out through an intermediary, usually a good friend of the older party.

At first, Hyun Jung wasn't impressed with Yung Hee. To Hyun Jung, Yung Hee's face looked too lumpy and dark, like a charcoal salesman, as they say. Her thin hairline was too far back, giving her an unusually high and wide forehead. Still, out of fear that she would be reprimanded if refused, Hyun Jung had, though reluctantly, acquiesced to be Yung Hee's little sister. Although they didn't buddy around much, Yung Hee played the role of a responsible older sister, all in all.

Ko Yung Hee stuck her head into Hyun Jung's room, then whispered, "Everyone must come to the dining hall."

"When?" Hyun Jung asked.

"Immediately."

When Hyun Jung stepped into the dining room, she saw two Communist soldiers. One was a head taller than the other. Each had a rifle hanging down from his shoulder. The shorter one pointed his rifle at the girls, who were sitting down with their eyes focused on the floor. The soldiers looked very young, maybe sixteen or seventeen. Like fresh converts, they were eager to show their newfound power and support for the Communist invaders by intimidating the girls.

"Where is everybody?" the shorter of the two soldiers demanded.

With pointed chins and shifty eyes, the young soldiers remarkably resembled each other. Their faded-green uniforms were covered with buttons showing photos of the Communist North Korea founder, Kim Il Sung. Red and gold stars decorated their shoulder pads and pockets.

The short soldier pounded on a little silvery bell that was kept on the long table for prayer calls before eating meals. He banged on the bell and said sarcastically, "You girls ring this bell and pray to God before eating your meals?"

No one spoke.

The soldier continued, "Isn't that right?" Still no one spoke, and the same soldier went on, "You all had a good life."

The girls just listened like captured prisoners and kept their eyes lowered to the floor.

"Where is everybody?" the soldier screamed. "You girls still don't know that your world has turned upside down now."

The other one looked at the girls and said, "Do you?"

Hyun Jung thought she could die any moment and quietly told herself, *Whatever happens, happens.*

The taller soldier joined up with the shorter guy to threaten the girls some more.

"We will take all the rice from you today. Only then, you girls will realize what's going on."

Still, no one spoke. The girls kept their eyes on the floor.

The same soldier continued his ranting, saying, "It's our turn to eat."

Then the two Communists stormed out of the dining hall and marched into the kitchen in the adjacent building.

They ordered the Kitchen Halmuhni, "Take us to the rice storage, old woman."

The Kitchen Halmuhni reluctantly showed them where the rice was kept. The two guys did not waste any time. They loaded all the rice, barley, beans, and other grains into their truck and sped away.

After watching the two Communists leave with all the grain they had, the Kitchen Halmuhni rushed over to the dining room. She was glad some girls were still there.

She told them what happened and cried with her mouth wide open, "I didn't know what to do!. They took all the rice, barley, and all the other grains. What do we do now?"

No one spoke.

The Kitchen Halmuhni continued, "What can we eat? They didn't even leave one handful of rice. They loaded all the rice into their truck and took off. What are we going to do?"

Hyun Jung, sitting at the far end of the long bench, was calm. She decided to face whatever might happen to her. *Even if death comes,* she thought, *you only die once.*

By late that afternoon, Principal Jo learned what happened at the dorm earlier. He immediately phoned Jung Joo Sill, the twelfth grader, for a meeting that evening. Joo Sill had been newly elected president of Ewha Girls' Middle School Student Body.

"Something very important," Principal Jo told Joo Sill over the phone.

Joo Sill brought her best girlfriend, Ko Yung Hee, with her to meet the Principal. The meeting took place at the far corner of the dorm's dining hall, where the two Communists had interrogated the Ewha girls earlier that afternoon.

Standing close together, Mr. Jo whispered to the two girls with his gestures for them to come closer, "Listen!" He looked around and continued in a hushed tone, "You know Ddook Ssuhm?"

"*Neh*?" Joo Sill asked. "Ddook Ssuhm, sir?"

The principal nodded. "The Han River Bridge has been bombed, you see," he said, searching the expression of the two girls standing close to him. "There is this old Boatman Grandfather," he continued. "He carries people across the Han River at Ddook Ssuhm. You know Ddook Ssuhm?" The two girls looked at him with a blank look. "It's the northernmost end of the Han River, farther out from the East Gate."

"Sir?" the girls asked, almost in unison.

"I want you all to leave."

"Yes?" Joo Sill said, with a surprised tone of voice. Yung Hee looked as surprised as Joo Sill did.

"Tomorrow," the principal continued, "I have arranged for the old Boatman Grandfather to help you over the river." He handed an envelope to Joo Sill and said, "Joo Sill, you be in charge. Bring a few more girls with you."

Joo Sill looked at Yung Hee's tense face and then took the envelope from the principal's hand.

"We don't have any rice to feed you girls anymore," Mr. Jo said. "There is no place to buy rice anywhere in the whole city. The rice merchants have closed their shops and fled the city. The soldiers who came earlier took all the rice, see?" The principal added in a whisper, "The government already bombed the Han River Bridge so the Communist soldiers couldn't cross." They nodded, and Mr. Jo added, "After crossing the river, go south. Continue on south; sooner or later you will meet up with the South Korean government. Understand?"

Joo Sill sucked in her breath and then replied, "Yes, sir."

The principal said, "Leave tomorrow morning. I will ask the Kitchen Halmuhni to cook your breakfast, early."

Ewha was fortunate to have a principal like Mr. Jo. He was one of the most caring principals ever, when it came to the welfare of the Ewha girls. He didn't spare anything. He was like their parents and grandparents, all meshed together. The girls at Ewha gave him a nickname, Grandfather Millet, for his way of paying attention to every aspect, big or small, of the Ewha girls and their welfare.

As soon as the principal left, Joo Sill turned to Yung Hee and said, "Let's pick a couple of girls to go with us."

Yung Hee was in deep thought.

Because she was the quiet type, she was popular among her peers. Joo Sill especially liked having Yung Hee as a close friend.

She said, "We have to do it right away. Get the ones who can keep up with us, walking every day, you know?"

"I know," Yung Hee said. "We don't have time to waste."

"We must take a couple of juniors," Joo Sill continued, "because they are old enough to keep up with us."

"How about Hyun Jung, my little sister?" Yung Hee asked.

"Oh," Joo Sill said. "But you know, she is too young. She will cry and hold us back." After a brief pause, she shook her head and said, "She won't do. No."

"But how can I leave my little sister behind?" Yung Hee pleaded. "I cannot do that."

Hyun Jung was sitting quietly on her bed in her newly assigned downstairs bedroom. No place to go and nothing to do. Then, suddenly, there was the thundering sound of airplanes swooping down. It sounded close enough to drop a bomb right on her head. She quickly crawled down under the bed, on the floor, face down, plugging her thumbs into her ears, and the rest of her hands covering her eyes, as she had learned from the gym teacher.

The evening of June 25 seemed like a long time ago, but only nine days had passed since that fateful day when they all had gathered in the gymnasium that had three small half-windows.

When she heard the thundering sound of the planes, Hyun Jung had dropped down, crawled under her bed, and began praying that it was an American bomber. *Please let it be an American plane.* She felt that an American bomber was the only hope for her in this suffocating world that had become a pure hell. Even after the sounds of the plane faded, she remained under the bed. She had to be sure the plane flew away, completely. When she was certain it was safe, she slowly began to wiggle out. Then she heard a soft knock on the door.

"Everything about America Was Good"

Hyun Jung was surprised to see Yung Hee, her *gyojae unnee* (Fellowship Sister), standing at the door.

"Oh, unnee [big sister]," Hyun Jung said, stepping aside to let Yung Hee in.

"I knocked, but you didn't answer," Yung Hee said. "Maybe you couldn't hear me because the planes were so loud."

"I am sorry, unnee … I was praying in there," Hyun Jung said, pointing to the floor under the bed. "Didn't hear you knock."

"Praying?"

"Yes," Hyun Jung said. "I was hoping the loud sounds were American planes."

"American planes?" she whispered. "But why?"

"That's the only hope we have."

Neither Yung Hee nor Hyun Jung had much contact with Americans, but they both believed everything about America was good, especially for South Korean people. Somehow, they knew.

"Hush," Yung Hee whispered, shaking her head. "We are leaving tomorrow, early in the morning."

"What?" Hyun Jung asked, confused. "Who's leaving tomorrow?"

"A group of us: two twelfth graders, Jung Joo Sill and myself, and two eleventh graders, Bae Jung Ja and Kim Keum Ja." Yung Hee then looked at Hyun Jung with a serious expression, as if she was in a deep thought. "They don't want to take you along."

Hyun Jung tilted her head, frowned, and confronted her unnee, "Why not? Why not take me along?"

"They said you were too young, and you will cry," Yung Hee replied. "They are afraid you will hold the group back."

Hyun Jung looked anxiously into Yung Hee's eyes and then said, "Oh, unnee, I won't cry. And I won't hold anyone back, I promise."

Yung Hee hesitated a bit and then asked, "Are you sure? But you are only thirteen years old, *kkoma* [kid]."

Hyun Jung didn't respond immediately; then, sounding determined, she said, "I promise I won't hold anyone back. I promise. Please let me come along."

Yung Hee felt sorry for Hyun Jung and finally accepted her request, saying, "Then, get ready. We'll be leaving early in the morning, right after breakfast."

"Oh, thank you, unnee."

"We will have breakfast in Kitchen Halmuhni's room."

This was the first meaningful encounter between the two girls since they had agreed to be sisters. Even after deciding to be fellowship sisters (*gyojae unnee* and *gyojae dongsaeng*), Yung Hee and Hyun Jung really didn't have much to do with each other.

Hyun Jung was well aware she had to obey the upperclassmen, Yung Hee and Joo Sill. But, Yung Hee was not very sociable to Hyun Jung. She would take Hyun Jung out shopping for clothes and took her to a restaurant to eat before coming back to the dorm. That's all. Hyun Jung had gone along because Yung Hee was the very first upperclassman to ask her to be her younger sister. Afterwards, she did her best to fill the role of being a good fellowship younger sister.

In this troubled time, Hyun Jung appreciated that Yung Hee didn't forget her. Actually, since no one from her own family came to save her at the school that day, Hyun Jung had been feeling abandoned by everybody, especially by her own family.

Everything had changed, even for the Kitchen Halmuhni and Grandpa. They had to share their living quarter with the girls. Since there were only sixteen girls in the dorm, the students had their meals where the Kitchen Halmuhni lived with her husband of forty-plus years.

The Kitchen Halmuhni and Grandpa were devoted to each other and took care of the girls at the dorm. Grandpa was a kind man and liked to help his wife. She worked hard cooking and looking after the girls, and he did errands around the dorm. He was half the size of his overweight wife, but his feelings toward her were big and genuine. They appeared to be contented to live on the school premises among the girls.

As long as there was rice and barley to cook, the old couple would scrape up *banchan* (side dishes), with wild plants like dandelions, mallow leaves, and wild onions growing wild in the schoolyard. But there was no more *bahp* (steamed rice), since the Communists emptied the grain bin yesterday.

As soon as Yung Hee left, Hyun Jung started to pack things in the same pink silk cloth she had taken with her when she walked to her home in the East Gate neighborhood. She packed the high-top brown leather shoes she had been saving for a special occasion, a framed photo of her family, and another framed photo of her father with Rhee Seung Mahn and half-dozen other Korean men that had been taken before Yu Chin San had fallen out with the president of the country. In addition, she packed the peach-colored American nylon dress her mother had bought for her that she had been saving and a pair of blue see-through nylon socks she had been saving to wear with the leather shoes. Nylon was newly introduced to Korea. The Korean people were fascinated by how easy the fabric was to take care of. They had been wearing cotton and silk for clothing, and they both required a lot of work to wash and iron to get the wrinkles out. On the other hand, nylon did not need ironing to get all the wrinkles out. The Korean mothers felt their work got easier because of the new American fabric. Another miracle of American invention, the Korean people thought.

The next morning, Kitchen Halmuhni and Grandpa scraped up some grain and potatoes for bahp (steamed grain). Grandma peeled the potatoes and then cut them into small pieces and cooked them with a handful of rice she had scraped up from the bottom of the rice barrel to stretch the dish further. For *banchan* (side dishes), as he often had done, Grandpa had gone out to the schoolyard and picked dandelions, mallow leaves, parrilla leaves, and wild onions. Halmuhni scalded the dandelion shoots and seasoned them with fermented bean paste, soy sauce, sesame seed oil, and minced garlic.

"Eat slowly, eat a lot," Kitchen Halmuhni said, wiping her eyes with her white apron. "*Aigoo*. You all have a long way to go."

No one spoke but continued with their breakfast.

"When will we see each other again?" The elderly Kitchen Halmuhni asked, breaking the silence and then turning her square head away to wipe her tears with her apron.

"Aren't you eating your breakfast, Halmuhni?" Hyun Jung asked.

Halmuhni didn't respond immediately but finally said, "Don't worry about me. You all must survive, hear?"

All the girls nodded. She wiped her eyes with the back of her hand and then said, "Yes," with a nod, between their chopsticks and spoon movements. "And find your parents," Kitchen Halmuhni said, covering her wrinkled face with her roughened-up brown hands and rushing out of the room to cry out loud.

The fresh scent from the ubiquitous purple lilac blossoms on the hilly Ewha campus sweetened the air as if nothing had changed. As the five girls got close to the school's main gate, Hyun Jung was surprised to see that the heavy gate was still left wide open, as if the school had been simply abandoned. The Gate Watchman Grandfather was nowhere to be seen.

"Oh, the Gate Watchman Grandfather must have already fled," Joo Sill said to Yung Hee, who was walking next to her.

Hyun Jung remembered how the gate had been wide open a few days before, when she walked to her house in Choong Shin Dong, in the East Gate neighborhood.

On July 5, exactly ten days after the Communist North invaded South Korea, one by one, the five Ewha girls quietly stepped out of the school's hilly campus. The eldest, twelfth graders Jung Joo Sill and Ko Yung Hee, went out of the gate first, then the two eleventh graders, Bae Jung Ja and Kim Keum Ja, followed. Finally, Yu Hyun Jung, the youngest, an eighth grader, took her turn. They all wore their school uniform: a knee-length navy-blue skirt and a white long-sleeved cotton blouse. Joo Sill was a head taller and bigger around than Yung Hee. The two eleventh graders, Bae Jung Ja and Kim Keum Ja, were the next. And, of course, Yu Hyun Jung, the eighth grader, was the smallest. The others often called Hyun Jung *kkoma* (kid).

The girls stepped out of the gate into the now-empty, deadly quiet street of Jung Dong, the very important neighborhood that housed many foreign and Korean government office buildings, including the Supreme Court. They walked quietly but briskly.

As the girls walked out of the school gate, Hyun Jung felt bad that Eun Ja couldn't come along. She knew the upperclassmen wouldn't agree to have one more kkoma tag along. Hyun Jung hoped Eun Ja would be safe. She also hoped they would see each other when they got back together again, soon.

After passing the Jung Dong Methodist Church on their right, they turned left to go to Jong Ro Boulevard. This was the same route Hyun Jung had taken a few days ago when she visited her home.

They walked past Duck Soo Palace on the right. The American Chancery and the Supreme Court buildings were nearby behind the wall, among the other important gray stone buildings.

It was quiet, with an eerie feeling, like walking around a graveyard. There was no sign of people anywhere. Hyun Jung wondered if they all had already fled the city or were hiding. She didn't even see the two Communist soldiers she saw a few days before.

All the shops on Jong Ro Boulevard were still closed. There were no moving vehicles in sight. Nothing had changed from the few days before when Hyun Jung had walked to her house. The whole city stopped moving, simply dead.

On Jong Ro Boulevard, the five Ewha girls continued walking toward the East Gate, as Principal Jo had told them to do. After a good two hours of walking, they passed Hyun Jung's old neighborhood, Choong Shin Dong, and headed to the far northeast upper tributary of the Han River, Ddook Ssuhm. They were simply following what the principal had instructed the two twelfth graders night before.

As they got closer to Ddook Ssuhm, the far end of town of the northeastern end of the Han River, white-clad refugees (Korean people are known to wear the color white) began to appear from all directions, like mushrooms after the rain. All, without exception, were heading in one direction: to the south to meet up with the South Korean government, away from the Communist North.

Hyun Jung followed the older girls without complaint, even when the planes were thundering above them. Joo Sill led the group, as Principal Jo had instructed. When they got to Ddook Ssuhm, they were to meet the old Boatman Grandfather.

However, when they finally arrived to where the old Boatman was supposed to be, he was nowhere to be seen. Hyun Jung saw Joo Sill and Yung Hee exchanging glances, as if to say, "Well? Where is he?"

Fleeing

In Geum San, about one hundred miles south of Seoul, alarmed town leaders got together to plot their survival.

Park Ki Taek, a stocky middle-aged man, arrived early to Peony, an all-night teahouse. First, he took time and surveyed the amber-colored room. Then, he picked a table away from where other people could hear their talk. He hoped all four of his men would show up soon. There was no time to linger, now the Communist North took Seoul, the capital city of the country.

As he waited, the willowy young waitress asked Park, "Would you care for some ginseng tea?"

Park hesitated a bit and then shook his head, saying, "I will wait until the others come." He then went back to glancing at his wristwatch.

Who would have guessed that supporting a candidate they knew had a good future would bring them bad fortune? Just less than two months before, supporting the woman candidate, Tae Jung Shin, appeared more advantageous than going with Yu Chin San. After all, Yu didn't even have a party; he was running as an independent. What could he do for them, even if they got him elected?

But who would have predicted that only forty-five days since their victorious election, the fate of the Republic of Korea, also known as South Korea, would be turned upside down? Now, with the Communists taking Seoul, the threat was fast spreading southward, like a forest fire on a windy day.

Around seven, when the bright June daylight yielded to the darkening of the early summer evening, the four men Park had been waiting for gathered around a corner table at the Peony Tea House. Each man knew the purpose of this evening's meeting. They were to plan their quiet and urgent escape from Geum San, the hometown where they were born, grew up, and prospered. That is, until they heard what happened to the capital city, Seoul, up north. Each of the men were certain they would be killed if they lingered and got captured by the Communist guerillas from the surrounding mountains.

This group of men had one thing in common: Each of them had fervently supported Tae Jung Shin, the American-educated woman candidate for the South Korean Parliament. In fact, she was the only woman candidate in the whole country and assumed to be very close to Rhee Seung Mahn, the president of the country. They were certain their status in the country would be bumped up once they got her elected, and endless fortune would follow.

"This is an emergency meeting," Park whispered to the other four, after they took their seats. "You all heard that Seoul is taken already."

Each man lowered his head. After searching the other four men's eyes, Park crushed his still-burning cigarette butt on the round bronze ashtray in front of him. He kept his voice low and added, "We don't have time and must act immediately."

"I hear you," Kwon, the eldest man in the group, said. "The Han River Bridge was already bombed by the government."

"Really?" Byun said, looking surprised.

"Hundreds of people were killed trying to cross," Kwon added, shaking his bald head.

Byun looked directly at Park and asked, "Have you tried to contact Congresswoman Tae?"

Park shook his head and said, "She's gone already to America, I am sure."

"Oh, no," Byun said. All the men shook their heads.

"Just like the Americans," Kwon said indignantly. "She only saves her own neck."

"We have to take off as soon as we can," Park said, looking at each man and then adding, "We don't have time to sit idle like this."

Lee, a chubby man in his late forties, said, "I agree, but …"

"Where to?" Byun asked.

"Follow the South Korean government, I guess," Kwon said. "What other choice do we have?"

Park said, "We will be dead meat when the *bbahl-gehng-ee* [Reds, Communists] put foot in this town. The government is now in Daejun, but who knows for how long?"

"President Rhee! That inept old man," Kwon said, shaking his head.

"Congresswoman Tae is no longer in Korea?" Lee asked, shaking his head. "She took off already?"

"What are you talking about? I already told you Daejun is taken," Kwon said impatiently. "How can Rhee Seung Mahn lose Seoul, the capital city, to the bbahl-gehng-ee?"

"We don't have time to waste. We need to gather a few more guys and take off before dawn," Park said. "The bbahl-gehng-ee guerillas are all over Ji Ri Mountain, as you all know." Park glanced at each man and then continued, "First, go south. We will aim for Daegu, okay?"

Everyone nodded without saying a word.

"And we'll try to get ahead of the government. They are busy being pushed down, you know. If this continues, before we know it, we'll all have to jump into *Dong Hae* [Eastern Sea], like chased lemmings."

"Without some connection in high places," Byun continued, "we cannot even get a spot to step in when we get to Daegu. I'm certain of that."

"Didn't I tell you not to attack Yu Chin San so much?" Kwon said.

Everyone lowered their heads.

"What good does it do to bring that up now?" Park snapped impatiently, as he crushed another of his cigarette butts in the ashtray.

"We went too far," Kwon continued. "Just because Tae had the backing of that old man, the president, and Yu was an independent with no money, we made all kinds of accusations to make him look bad."

"Again, what good does it do to say all that now?" Park asked. "What's done is done." He looked up at Lee and said, "Lee, what do you say? How about quietly getting some more guys to come along?"

He took a list of names from his breast pocket, handed it to Lee, and whispered, "We simply have to find ways to survive."

Everyone nodded in agreement.

"Look, Byun," Park said. "Everyone must be ready to take off early in the morning, before dawn. Help Lee, will you? We can have fifteen. You pick them, quietly. We cannot take any family members. You all know that," Park said. "Don't you?"

Everybody nodded except Lee.

"Why not?" he asked.

"They will kill us guys first."

"So what can we do? Walk?"

"Yeah, walk."

"What choice do we have?"

"We are the prime targets for the bbahl-gehng-ee."

"Don't tell anyone, not even your children, that we are taking off," Park said. "We have to sneak out when it's still dark and no one can see us." He looked around and whispered, "Understand?"

"I will tell my wife to make some rice balls and put them in a large bag," Kwon said.

"I will bring some kimchi," Lee said. "My wife makes the best kimchi."

With the strong backing of President Rhee, Tae Jung Shin got elected to the Congress. *Her election would have guaranteed all these men cushy government positions in Geum San,* Kwon thought, *or even, in Seoul. However, she chose to save only her own neck without so much as a word to anyone before taking off.*

"She abandoned everyone after getting elected," Lee said.

"Where do we go?" Byun asked.

"What do you mean, where?" Park asked back.

"We only have one place, the place where the South Korean government is, or soon will be. We don't have any choice," Kwon said, peering into the dark, frightened eyes of these men, who were in their prime years—forties through early sixties.

Lee said, "I heard the government is already running away from Daejun and heading south, towards Daegu."

"That's what I heard too," Byun said.

"You mean we are going to walk all the way to Daegu?" Kwon asked. "That's over one hundred miles from here."

"Our days are marked," Park said, looking at everyone around the table. "We just have to stick together and get to wherever the South Korean government is. That's our only choice."

"Of course," Kwon said. "We cannot just sit here and get killed by the damn bbahl-gehng-ee."

"Who will help us? We have no one to turn to in Daegu," Byun said, looking around all the men at the table with their heads down.

That night, while the whole town was still asleep, the fifteen men quietly snuck out of their homes and out of Geum San, where they had been on the top of the heap and occupying enviable positions. Now, the situation had turned upside down. The only choice for these men was going to a strange place. In fact, no one in the group had been to North Kyongsang Province, where the people spoke a strange dialect. Daegu is the capital city, but none of the fifteen men had ever been there before. The big obstacle was that no one knew anyone to turn to for help, when they got there.

10

Looking for the Boatman

Under a balmy cobalt-blue sky, the old boatman had been waiting for the Ewha students to show up. Just yesterday, Principal Jo had promised him they would come around the noon. However, when the thunderous fighter jets swooped down, he ran for his life. He rushed behind the tallest shrubs he could see and hid his thin body, with both arms covering his small head. Even though it was wartime, the Boatman kept himself busy carrying the refugees over to the south side of the Han River tributary.

"*Halahbuhjee* [Grandfather]," Joo Sill hollered, to get the attention of the old boatman when she first spotted him rushing toward the girls.

"The planes were so loud ... Aigoo!, I am having a hard time," the Boatman Grandfather said, walking closer to the five girls. I am glad you girls waited. I was afraid you might have thought I wasn't here. In fact, I was waiting for you to show up all morning."

He was tall and thin, with a leathery, sunbaked, copper-brown face under a tattered, wide-brimmed straw hat. "Principal Jo told me to expect you students," he said. Then, he peered around suspiciously to make sure no one else could hear him.

Joo Sill quietly took out the white envelope Principal Jo had given her the night before and handed it over to the Boatman Grandfather. Without even opening the envelope, he tucked it away in his money belt and then motioned with his pointed chin for the five girls to follow him to his boat. He made sure all the girls got onto the motorboat. Then, by steadying the boat with two long poles, the boatman began rowing across the narrow mouth of the upper Han River tributary.

The Boatman Grandfather glanced up at the sky. Hyun Jung knew he was making sure no planes were swooping down again. Each of the girls held her little bag tightly up against her bosom. The fates would take them wherever it would go.

As long as it took them southward, Hyun Jung thought.

Without saying a word to anyone, the old boatman quietly brought the five girls across to the south side of the Han River.

When his boat reached close to the south side of the shore, the Boatman Grandfather carefully slowed the boat down by steading it with his pole. He then helped each girl get off his still-toggling boat.

Looking up at the sky, he commented, "I wish I knew what those planes are up to."

No one responded to the old boatman. They didn't even look at each other, instead concentrating on stepping out from the still-moving boat. The old man and the five girls shared the same question: What were the planes trying to do?

The first thing that caught Hyun Jung's attention after she landed on the south side of the Han River was the stream of white-clad people, Korean people, scared people, running away from what had happened to them only ten days before. All were walking in the same direction: south. Hyun Jung thought, *Toward the south, where they believed their government would be.* There were no guarantees, however, that they would be safe when they got there. The alternative of not running away, however, was worse: sure death by the hands of the cruel Communist invaders.

The narrow two-lane gravel road was the only path available for the scared Korean people running for their lives. Hyun Jung saw a man carrying a white-haired old Halmuhni on his coolie rack, struggling. *Oh, his poor back,* Hyun Jung thought. She saw several people carrying their belongings on their backs, even on their heads. She also saw a family of four, the man carrying a child on the very top of his coolie rack, saying loudly, "Hold on tight. If you don't, you will die, hear? Hold on tight."

Next to the man were two women: one middle-aged and an older grandmother. They rushed their steps while holding each other's hands, as if someone was expecting to greet them when they got wherever they were going.

With their quiet footsteps, the five Ewha girls joined the flow of refugees. In the midst of the thick wave of people, Hyun Jung spotted two Communist soldiers on horseback, approaching them. At first, the girls pretended they didn't see them and kept walking. As Hyun Jung glanced sideways at the soldiers, she noticed their shoulder badges. They were covered with pictures of Kim Il Sung's full face, red and blue with a white star, and North Korean Communist flags.

One of the soldiers came near the Ewha girls and asked, "Where are you all going, comrades?"

The five girls all stopped walking and looked at their leader, Joo Sill, to speak for them.

"Next town, sir," she answered.

The soldier then said, "We are all in one country now, comrades."

Joo Sill paused and then said, "Our homes are right in the next town, sir."

With no further question, the two soldiers moved on.

The Ewha girls resumed their walking. They knew they had a long way to go.

Just as Hyun Jung caught her breath, she heard a loud thundering sound from the mountain above. She looked up to the sky and saw black marks, like crosses. They were fast approaching towards them, looking like a pack of eagles swooping down to grab a fish. As they flew down, she bent forward and protected herself with both hands covering her face.

All the Ewha girls covered their ears with their thumbs and their eyes with the rest of their hands, as they had been taught at their school gym, on the night of June 25, that fateful first night of the invasion. The girls dropped themselves onto the gravel and remained down until after the planes flew away, into the high cloudless sky.

One by one, the girls brought themselves up and immediately began brushing the dirt from their arms, from their navy-blue skirts, and from their long-sleeved blouses. Immediately, they surveyed the road, which was still packed with refugees, and resumed their walking.

Yung Hee went over to Hyun Jung and asked, "Are you okay?"

Hyun Jung nodded and replied, "*Neh*" [Yes, ma'am].

Yung Hee told Hyun Jung, "The Communists are trying to make friends with us now, trying to win us over."

"Really?" Hyun Jung asked.

"That's why they were not mean to us," she said, "because they are winning the war, for now. They might change; who knows? Be careful. A full-fledged fight is going on up the hill; you hear the cannon blasts and gunshots, don't you?"

As it was supposed to be, they still walked in seniority order, even when walking close to a battlefield: Joo Sill and Yung Hee, the twelfth graders, first at the front, followed by the two eleventh graders, Jung Ja and Keum Ja. They walked together side by side. Hyun Jung tried to keep up with the upper classmen, but walked behind them because she didn't have anyone her age to walk with; she missed Eun Ja.

If the sea of white-clad people heading south looked like moving ocean waves, the constant sound of cannon blasts from the nearby battlefield reminded them that they were, in fact, in a war zone. The only thing they could do now was to put one foot ahead of the other and keep walking, until they met up with the now-fleeing South Korean government, wherever and whenever that might be. Hyun Jung wondered if the walking would ever end, but it was only the first day of their long journey of fleeing the Communist invaders.

As they began walking uphill, they noticed some soldiers coming down the mountain. Several of them had arm slings, and some were being carried down in stretchers and gurneys. No one talked. Everyone pretended not to see anything. They simply continued walking.

The air smelled of blood. From time to time, the sounds of cannon blasts from the nearby mountains reminded them the fighting was going on, up there, nearby, and the girls had no choice but to continue walking, southward, in the same direction they believed their government had fled to.

Hyun Jung walked as fast as she could. She was determined not to get behind and slow the group down. At one point, she walked so quickly she moved right next to Yung Hee and Joo Sill, ahead of the two eleventh graders.

Hyun Jung saw Joo Sill glance at her and tell Yung Hee, "The kkoma [kid] referring to Hyun Jung, "is doing alright so far. She is not holding us back, as I was afraid that she might."

"Of course not," Yung Hee answered bluntly. "What did I tell you? She might be a kkoma, but she's determined."

"I know," Joo Sill said. "You said she would give us no trouble, but I wasn't too sure. I am glad she is keeping up so far; of course, it's only the first day."

"She will be no problem, I assure you," Yung Hee said. "She knows she has to keep up with us."

Just then, Joo Sill and Yung Hee made a sudden stop and looked to their left, to the other side of the refugee-packed road. Hyun Jung followed suit. She noticed a man approaching her group from across the road. He appeared to be with three other people, who remained on the other side of the road. He was coming towards them, alone.

11

Kim Tae Young from Ahn Dong

The man stopped when he came close to the Ewha girls. For a Korean man, he was tall and fair-skinned. "Are you girl students walking by yourselves?" he asked when he got closer.

Joo Sill, looking straight at him, though reluctantly, answered, "Yes."

"Oh, I'm sorry," the man said. "My name is Kim Tae Young."

"Yes," Joo Sill repeated. "Why?" she then asked firmly. "Is there a problem?"

"Won't you join us?" he answered. "It's dangerous for young girls to walk by themselves. We are heading for Ahn Dong." He glanced at his entourage across the road.

With a quick glance, Joo Sill surveyed her group. All the girls silently nodded yes.

The man signaled his group to come over and join up with the girls. There were four people in his group: one woman and three men. Mr. Kim seemed to be the eldest and the leader of the group.

Hyun Jung felt much better having these adults walking along. It was stressful for them to be alone, without any adults. *Mr. Kim's group appeared harmless, even, rather cultivated*, Hyun Jung thought.

There was nothing to fear in joining up with them. Everybody knew the city, Ahn Dong in North Kyung Sang Do. Ahn Dong was well-known among the Korean people for its inhabitants, mainly composed of descendants of *yangban* (aristocrats).

The only woman in Mr. Kim's group appeared to be a wife of a high-level officer in the South Korean government or a professor at a university. Lady Cha had a headful of dark brown wavy hair that was sprinkled with gray above her wide, brown-rimmed glasses. Her face was narrow and clean. She didn't speak to the girls but greeted them with a nod and soft smile. Besides Kim Tae Young, there were two younger men: Moon Young Ho, who was slim and wore glasses, and Song Jung Sik, a short man who looked to be the youngest.

The nine people from Seoul resumed walking together. The two-lane gravel road headed south was still packed with refugees. Some carried pots and pans on their back-racks.

Some were holding young children by their hands. Still others carried their belongings on their heads. No one talked, but the wave of refugees continued on, one foot in front of the other, in the same direction, to the south, away from the Communist invaders and where the fleeing South Korean government supposedly had relocated. There were no vehicles with wheels, not even bicycles, to help carry them away farther from the invaders from the North.

Silence was broken, from time to time, by gunshots coming from the nearby mountains above. As the group walked up the hilly side of a steep mountain, a stream of wounded soldiers passed in the opposite direction. Some of them were being carried down on stretchers, and some walked holding their bandaged arms. This scene reminded Hyun Jung that the fighting was going on really close by. In fact, they might be in the middle of a battle zone.

Hyun Jung was still mindful of not dragging her group behind. She followed close to the adults, especially Mr. Kim, now the group leader. She was glad to have the safety of nine people, and grown-ups, too. Having the three men who were older and having Lady Cha made Hyun Jung feel safer. She almost breathed a sigh of relief.

But the feeling of safety was short-lived. As they were walking up the road by tall July green grass, Hyun Jung looked up and saw something like a black cross in the sky. Before she could turn her head back, she heard a loud thundering sound. It felt like it could tear up her eardrums. The five Ewha girls immediately dropped to the roadside, plugged both ears with their thumbs, and covered their eyes with their hands as they were taught to do that night by their gym teacher, Chang.

Everybody remained on the ground until the planes disappeared and the noise completely faded away. Then the girls pulled themselves up. It was frightening to look at each other's dirt-smeared faces and clothes. They helped each other to brush the dirt off from their cheeks, arms, blouses, and navy-blue skirts.

"You all knew what to do when the planes swooped down, didn't you?" Mr. Kim remarked.

"Our gym teacher taught us what to do times like this, when the planes would drop bombs on us," Joo Sill explained.

"That's so good of the teacher," Lady Cha remarked.

12

Into a Culvert at Gunpoint

Hyun Jung followed the others while being mindful of the sound of gunfire coming from the top of the nearby mountains. She eyed the wounded soldiers who were quietly being carried down on stretchers and gurneys, while more soldiers walked down wearing arm slings. A few were using crutches.

No one spoke.

The girls hadn't eaten since that early breakfast Kitchen Halmuhni cooked for them before they left their dorm. But the thought of food didn't even enter their minds. They knew what was going on up on the nearby mountain. They didn't need to get any closer to the battlefield to know what was happening. They could imagine the bloody battles going on.

Mr. Kim looked back to make sure his group was still intact. Quietly, as if nothing had happened, he steadily put one foot ahead of the other. Finally, they came to a low land where the patches of dark green grass were so tall they almost came up to their waists.

Just then, all of a sudden, everyone heard a strong male voice yell, "Stop!"

Two Communist soldiers sprang up from the tall summer grass. They pointed their rifles at the nine refugees. Everyone immediately stopped walking and waited for a signal from their leader.

"Get in," one of the soldiers commanded, pointing at a nearby culvert with his rifle. Mr. Kim didn't say anything. He just followed the order.

Bending their heads, everyone followed the leader into a damp culvert. The inside of the culvert was not completely dark. Rather, it was the color of dark brown, the color of brownish burnt umber.

One of the soldiers went to the back of the group to make sure each and all persons got into the culvert. One by one, all nine of the refugees from Seoul, still keeping their eyes down, took seats on dirt ground inside the culvert, with their backs up against the damp cement wall.

It was quiet, deadly quiet. The only sound Hyun Jung heard was the trickling sound of water flowing a couple of feet away from her feet.

Inside the culvert, the two Communist soldiers took turns guarding the group with guns pointed towards the group. They spoke in quiet mumbles, only to each other. Finally, they took seats on the opposite side, directly facing the group.

Still, no one spoke. They were fearful of creating any provocation. Hyun Jung noticed the shadows and light at the opposite end of the culvert. At one point, she noticed some light at the far end of the culvert.

The July afternoon sun was at its full force. She kept watching the sunlight at the far end of the tunnel. As her eyes wandered to the light, and back again, and back to the trickling water, so close to her toes, she noticed there was no more sunlight, even at the opposite end. From inside of the culvert, the outside looked the color of faded beige.

Still, no one spoke inside the culvert. It was as if there were no living human beings around. Everyone was afraid to have their eyes meet with the soldiers. They just kept their gaze focused on the ground.

Each person waited for a signal from the leader. Hyun Jung glanced over at Lady Cha, who stared out of the little hole at the other end of the culvert. Hyun Jung assumed the sun was lingering on, preparing itself for disappearance. In the damp culvert, the hours appeared to have stopped. Who knew how long the two young Communist soldiers had been hiding there? They could have been deserters. But they had guns with them, and therefore, they had the power to harm or even kill each member of the group.

After ordering the nine refugees into the culvert, the two soldiers said nothing, but their sharp eyes watched every move the people in front of them made. No one talked. The only sound was the hollow noise of water flowing through the culvert. The sun finally began to disappear toward the west, and the sky slowly turned the color of lifeless beige and began to change to dark brown.

Hyun Jung could tell by the subdued yellow and brown light outside the opposite end of the culvert that the day was nearly over. She also noted a large boulder at the opposite end of the culvert. The sun weakened in the west, but no one dared to make a single remark, not even a sound. The nine refugees from Seoul sat with their eyes lowered. They were worried what could happen if their eyes were to meet up with the eyes of the vigilant two Communist soldiers. Hyun Jung kept her mind occupied watching the little minnows in the flowing water. The school of fish were playing in the shallow water. Hyun Jung envied the minnows in the stream. At least they were not afraid the soldiers might gun them down with a slightest provocation.

Although it had been only ten days since the Communists invaded Seoul, to Hyun Jung, it seemed like it had been years. One moment, she and the other girls were protected at Ewha, living on the secure campus with a Watchman Grandfather to guard them from anything that could harm them. But now, they feared for their lives, not knowing if they'd be gunned down. The world had turned upside down for them. No one knew about tomorrow or even ten minutes from now. Their lives didn't appear to have any value. They now were disposable, at the whim of these two young soldiers sitting so close, directly across from them. The soldiers had power over every one of the nine because their guns were loaded. The two Communists soldiers were able to use the guns on any one of the people in the culvert in this time of war.

The nine refugees from Seoul, without exception, kept their heads down. Their fears were real. The safest thing to do was to go along with whatever the soldiers wanted. They could not walk anymore and planned to go to sleep when the sun set. They would get up and begin walking again if the soldiers set them free. Food? What's that? No one dwelled on eating or hunger; surviving was more important than having food.

At the opposite end, Hyun Jung could see some changes took place. The sun had been bright and lemon yellow when they first walked into the culvert. But now, Hyun Jung watched the slow-changing shadow on the big boulder she had spotted at the end of the culvert on the opposite side from the entrance. The boulder had a well-defined crack line, and when they entered the culvert, it had been half in shadow and half in sunlight. Now, the rock, mostly a light shadow of taupe with a very small area at the far left side, was turning dark gray.

Still, no one looked at the other, fearing that might provoke the soldiers into using their rifles.

The sun was finally setting, and the sky turned dark gray. Hyun Jung watched the staccato movements of the minnows in the tiny, clear pool of water by her feet. Her eyes followed the fish in the shallow puddle of the water. She envied the carefree minnows. *They have more life and freedom than I do,* she thought.

Suddenly, in what appeared to be late afternoon, or early evening, without a word to anyone, the two Communist soldiers stooped their heads and walked out of the culvert.

No one said anything or made a move for a long time.

13

House on the Hill

"The soldiers are gone," Mr. Kim whispered, looking around his newfound group. "We must be alone." Then he looked at each member and said, "Let's get out of here. It's getting dark."

"Let's see what we can find," Moon said.

The rest of the group followed the two men out of the culvert, where they had spent the good part of the day.

"Maybe some food," Song said, stretching his arms above his head.

Lady Cha asked around, "When was the last time you all had anything to eat?"

Joo Sill answered, "This morning, at dawn, ma'am, before we left our dorm."

One by one, the refugees followed Mr. Kim out of the damp culvert, where they had been kept for most of the long July summer day. Their leader climbed a narrow path up the hill as soon as he stepped out of the culvert. Moon followed up the meandering and narrow hillside road. And the rest of the group followed and climbed the steep hill. After struggling to stay on the narrow path, they came to a rather large farmhouse with a thatched roof. It was sitting snugly alone on top of the small hill. Like many Korean rural village farmhouses, it was surrounded by vegetable gardens, but there were no signs of people.

"You all wait here while Moon and I go up and check it out," Mr. Kim said, motioning for Moon to come along. The two men continued up the hill. When they finally reached the front gate of the house, they hollered, "*Yu- bo- se-yo?*" [Hello, anybody home? Hello.] When no one answered, they pushed through the gate. A few minutes later, Moon came out and motioned for the rest of the group to come on up.

The house, with its well-swept front yard, reminded Hyun Jung of her own home in Jin San. She felt sad and briefly thought how she missed her mother's kindly, wrinkle-covered face.

The only signs of life at the farmhouse were plump brown and orange chickens scurrying around with excitement when the two men entered the house. It was obvious that the owners of the house ran for their lives when they first heard the Communists had invaded the South and Seoul had fallen into the hands of the Communists, and they were coming down southward. They must have known they wouldn't be safe, if caught by the Communists.

It was getting dark, and the group had to find some food before it got too late.

"It's clean," Joo Sill said loudly.

The two men and Lady Cha looked around the house for some rice. Mr. Kim was happy to discover plenty of rice in a large earthenware barrel in the kitchen.

"I see a large container of delicious kimchi," Lady Cha said, with a big smile.

Song said loudly, "Now, we have everything!"

Leader Kim said, "Boil some water in a big pot, please." Lady Cha repeated it to Joo Sill and Yung Hee, who were standing a few feet away.

Song said, with a big grin, "Plenty of rice and a ton of kimchi. Now we have everything!" He continued, "Tonight, we'll eat until our stomachs are full. There is no better heaven!"

"They left everything behind," Mr. Kim said. "It looks like they just took off."

Song began to chase the chickens, while Joo Sill and Yung Hee put a large pot of water on the fire.

After much effort, Song grabbed a large and loudly protesting orange chicken. He then held the neck firmly before giving it a vigorous twist. The chicken continued protesting, kicking its feet and loudly croaking. Song, however, persevered. His grip was firm until the bird took its last gasp with blank, dark eyes. He did the same with a second chicken and then handed them to Moon, who was eager to assist him, while the rest were simply getting out of the way. They caught two more chickens.

"We'll take some with us tomorrow," Lady Cha said.

Moon joyfully dunked the birds into the boiling hot water and then put them in a large metal tub. The two young men immediately started to pull all the feathers off the chickens. After they finished plucking the feathers, Mr. Kim slit the stomachs open with a sharp kitchen knife.

"Aigoo," Yung Hee lamented, glaring at Joo Sill. "Their nerves are still twitching in every second like the hands of a clock, see?"

"Here, let me have it," Joo Sill said, taking the plucked chickens and yanking out the guts and gizzards to wash them before putting the chickens back into the boiling water.

"I became a vegetarian after I saw that happen before," Yung Hee said, turning her head away from the dismantling of the chickens.

That night, without saying a word, the whole group, nine all together, sat at the kitchen table and feasted on chicken stew, steamed rice, and plenty of sweet and spicy kimchi.

With full stomachs, they spent the night at the house. The women slept in a separate bedroom that had an oiled, shiny golden paper floor. What a change. Even though they were sleeping on the floor, it was so much better than the culvert, where they had spent the whole day earlier.

Early the next morning, the nine refugees from Seoul got up and had breakfast with the most delicious leftovers they could remember ever having.

"How lucky we are," Moon said, with a grin. "I am glad the two young soldiers didn't find this house and eat up all the chicken and kimchi before we came up."

Everybody nodded in agreement.

"Yeah, I agree," Song said, and everyone nodded.

"No one knows when we will eat again," Keum Ja said.

"Yeah, we should make some rice balls to take with us," Lady Cha said. "We still have a long way to go."

Joo Sill and Yung Hee both readily agreed and began preparing the rice balls.

Smell of Blood

It was another hot July day. While conscious of the cannon blasts and gunshots from nearby battlefields, the group resumed their southward flight. The nine refugees lined up behind Mr. Kim and started walking down the meandering, narrow, and steep passageway to the main highway below.

When they finally reached the main road, Hyun Jung noticed a number of wounded soldiers heading down. As it did yesterday, the endless waves of white-clad refugees again covered the highway.

Other than the soldiers, the road looked the same as it did the day before. The people wore varying shades of white and carried as much as they could on their backs and heads . Some were holding their child's hand, rushing southward as if somebody was waiting to greet them when they finally met up with the South Korean government.

On the side of the main road, Mr. Kim stopped and waited for everyone to gather around him.

"Which direction shall we take?" Lady Cha asked him.

"We should get away from this main highway," he said. "This road is so packed with refugees and wounded soldiers."

"I cannot stand the smell of blood anymore," Kim Keum Ja said, shaking her head and wrinkling her nose.

"Maybe we can see what's over there," Mr. Kim said, gesturing toward a massive mountain to the west of the highway.

"And climb that tall mountain?" Joo Sill asked, staring at the leader and shaking her head.

"Do you have a better suggestion?" he asked.

Lady Cha looked worried and said, "Oh, no."

"Such a tall mountain to climb," Yung Hee mumbled to herself.

As they continued to walk, the mountain grew more massive and looked as though it would devour all nine people.

Still, Mr. Kim led his group away from the crowded main highway and toward the mountain. As they followed their leader over the narrow wall of rice terraces, he spotted the dark line of a wide river ahead.

"Oh, no," he lamented loudly when he first spotted the trembling waters. "I didn't see that from the road. It's flowing rather rapidly. And the mountain is so tall and towering." Mr. Kim looked up, shook his head, and said with disbelief, "Wow!"

"It's still better than being squeezed amongst the endless line of refugees on the packed highway," Song said. "Who knows what's on the other side of the mountain?"

Everyone nodded.

"I will go first and check it out," Song offered. "Kkoma, come with me?"

Hyun Jung was happy to get Song's attention.

The rest of the group followed the leader in complete silence. Moon Young Ho helped Lady Cha, who was struggling to stay on the narrow rice terrace.

When Song stopped at the edge of the rice terrace and saw the wide, swiftly flowing river, he was taken aback and said simply, "Wow! So big! The water is so dark, cold, and green. Still, better than the refugee-packed highway."

Song and Hyun Jung made a quick survey of the river and went back to the group to report. Hyun Jung was glad for the chance to be helpful to the group.

"Look, it's a large river," Song said, reaching his arms toward Hyun Jung. "Didn't see it from the road, but we'll have to cross it, somehow."

Each and every person knew what Song was saying and followed the leader without saying anything. When they came close to the river, Kim Keum Ja said, "It's dark and cold-looking ... swift too!"

"It won't be too bad," Song said. "Kkoma and I looked at it. Let's just start. We don't have a choice if we want to find a road with fewer refugees and make to the other side of the mountain."

Mr. Kim took his shoes off and rolled his trouser legs up while glancing to see how the others were doing. Lady Cha shortened her skirt by rolling up its waistband. She then took off her shoes. All the girls copied Lady Cha and shortened their skirts by rolling up their waistbands.

Mr. Kim started into the water first.

"Wow," he cried. "It's icy cold."

As Lady Cha stepped into the river, she stumbled and slipped on a rock. Mr. Kim rushed to help her up, and then they walked across the river together.

Holding their bags up on their heads with one hand, and hugging their shoes against their bosoms, the five Ewha girls cautiously began walking into the cold river.

Song reached out to lend a hand to Hyun Jung. She appreciated his attention. Actually, she liked him, a lot. He seemed nice and was almost old enough to be her older brother, Joong Yul. Briefly, Hyun Jung remembered her brother's broad face, but she had no idea where he was now. For that matter, she didn't have the time to reminisce about such luxury subjects like family and their safety, as she wasn't sure whether she herself would be alive a minute from then.

The water was green, cold, and dark as it flowed swiftly southward. It was important to cross the rough river safely. The water came up to Lady Cha's waist. When she made to the other side of the river, the girls watched, with awe, as she began bravely climbing up to the mountain. The girls put their little bags and shoes on top of their heads while holding onto them with one hand, balancing with the other hand.

Mr. Kim stepped back to help Lady Cha, and they continued climbing in front of the group. Everyone wobbled left and right to keep up with their elders. Finally, after great tribulations, the two elders crossed the river and started up the mountain.

As for the rest of the group, when they made it to the riverbank at the foot of the mountain, they felt they were finally safe.

"Look at me," Keum Ja said. "I am soaked." She wrung the water out from her dripping navy-blue skirt.

"Aigoo," Yung Hee cried. "I am scared, but everybody seemed so brave!"

"The mountain is towering," Joo Sill exclaimed. *"Aigoo!"*

"We don't have the time to worry. Hurry, begin the climb," Yung Hee said loudly and began struggling upwards. The group from Seoul began climbing the steep mountain, holding on to bushes, small tree branches, whatever they could reach with bare hands. Hyun Jung grabbed the branch of a bush to pull herself up, but the twigs broke off, and she slipped. Song rushed down to help. Yung Hee looked back to make sure her little sister was all right, then turned around to resume walking up the steep mountain.

"What's the matter?" Song asked Hyun Jung. "Here, give me your hand." Hyun Jung reached her hand out, and he pulled her up. "You're such a good kid; you haven't even cried once."

"Well, I promised my sister I wouldn't cry," Hyun Jung said, holding her bag even more tightly.

"Yeah?" Song asked. "Who's your sister?"

"She is ahead of us," Hyun Jung said. "She made me promise I wouldn't cry and hold the group back."

"Aren't you a brave young lady?" Song said, helping Hyun Jung up.

Before anyone knew, Jung Ja, one of the eleventh graders, slid down the slippery mountain path, almost to the riverbank below. Moon happened to notice what was going on. He immediately rushed back down and offered to carry her on his back up the hill. In the meantime, Hyun Jung slipped again. Song rushed down and rescued her.

"I'll be fine," she said, shaking her head lightly. "Go, help *unnee*s, big sisters."

"Just let me have your hand, then."

Song was more than willing to help the youngest in the group. She held his hand tightly and pulled herself up. This was the first time Hyun Jung had ever held a man's hand. She was truly grateful for Song's help. The dwarf shrubs that dotted the mountain landscape were too flimsy to pull up on.

"Aigoo," Yung Hee lamented.

Having reached the top of the mountain, Lady Cha and Mr. Kim took a break and congratulated each other for making it to the peak.

"For a woman your age," the leader said, "you are strong."

"Thanks," Lady Cha said, "but I am not the only one."

After complimenting each other, they found a spot to sit down and relax while waiting for the group to make it up to the top.

"I know," Mr. Kim said. "We have some good people in our group."

"That's right," she agreed, adding, "Very. Let's sit down here and relax for a while." She had spotted a relatively flat grass-covered area where they could sit down.

"That *kkoma* is keeping up with us okay, I believe," Mr. Kim said.

"She seems like a determined young girl," Lady Cha replied. "Song's paying a lot of attention to her."

"That's good. They need to help each other."

"She appears to be a resolute little girl, though."

"I noticed that too."

"She was determined not to get left behind, I guess. I hope everyone makes it up before it gets too dark."

The Leader spotted a relatively flat grass-covered area and sat his tired body down.

"Should we spend the night here?" Lady Cha asked the leader.

He nodded, and they continued to wait for the others.

They were grateful no one had gotten hurt so far. While waiting for the rest of the group to make it to the top, Mr. Kim cleared the area, and Lady Cha, welcoming the opportunity to rest, dropped herself down.

"I wonder how far we have to walk before reaching the South Korea side," Mr. Kim said. "Honestly, I am not even sure which side we are on now."

Lady Cha replied, "There is no way to tell. One thing I know, and that is the government went southward, away from the Northern invaders, you know."

A brief silence followed.

"How did the president let things get so out of hand?" Mr. Kim mumbled, shaking his head.

"That's what I say too," Lady Cha said in a hushed tone of voice.

"They took the capital city so swiftly," he added.

After a brief pause, Lady Cha stated soberly, "That old man's got to go" (referring to President Rhee Seung Mahn).

Getting to Know You

Night was fast approaching when all nine refugees from Seoul finally reached the top of the sky-high mountain.

Moon looked around the mountaintop and said, "Yeah, maybe we should sleep up here tonight."

"Better than sleeping on the side of a road or in a culvert," Mr. Kim said.

"It's getting late," Lady Cha said. "There's no guarantee we'd find a better spot for tonight."

After the ordeal they had been through crossing the river and climbing the lofty mountain, the adjacent barley field on the top of the mountain looked harmless, even inviting.

"I don't hear any gunshots," Song said, with a smile.

"Yes, let's stay here tonight and start early in the morning," Ko Yung Hee agreed.

Hyun Jung appreciated that she didn't have to leave the beautiful place so soon after getting up there. The blue sky was so beautiful seeping through the pine tree branches. Hyun Jung had never seen this before. Everyone was quite taken with the peaceful scenery from the top of the mountain. The sky turned purple, orange, gray, and even more colors.

Mr. Kim softly whispered, "I think we are on the South Korean side."

Everyone nodded.

Yung Hee tried to make a spot for her little sister, Hyun Jung. "Here," she said. "Come sit down next to me."

Lady Cha and Joo Sill passed out the rice balls they had brought with them from the farmhouse where they had cooked and ate supper and spent the last night. After eating the rice balls, everyone relaxed a bit, far from the Communist invaders. They were now safe on top of the tall mountain.

"It's good that we brought these," Lady Cha said, holding up one of the rice balls.

Mr. Kim nodded thoughtfully. He then looked at each person in the group and said, "We have been together for two whole days now, but we have not even introduced ourselves."

"That's right," Lady Cha concurred.

"We are going to Andong," Mr. Kim said, sitting down in the flat spot he swept clear for himself. "Where are you students headed? Where are your homes?"

Following a short pause, Joo Sill answered, "My home is in Busan, but Yung Hee, who is going with me, is from Kang Won Do."

"Kang Won Do?" Lady Cha said, raising her voice with a surprised look. "She cannot go there, now."

"Of course not," Moon said, "Kang Won Do is already taken, as you all know."

No one spoke for a while. The mood quickly turned rather somber.

"How about the others?" Lady Cha asked, softening her tone.

Joo Sill said, "These two, Keum Ja and Jung Ja, are from Mokpo, in South Chula Do."

"Mokpo?" Lady Cha asked. "I wonder if the guerillas there have charged up now? After invading Seoul, they may try to take over."

When no one responded, Joo Sill continued, "And kkoma is from Jin San, in South Choong Chung Do, south of Daejun."

"Daejun is already taken too, you know," Mr. Kim said.

"She can go with us to Daegu and find her father," Ko Yung Hee said.

"That kkoma," Joo Sill said. "She is one determined kid."

"Trying to find her father?" Mr. Kim asked.

Ko Yung Hee nodded and then whispered, "Chairman Yu Chin San."

"Chairman Yu Chin San?" Mr. Kim repeated, alarmed.

Joo Sill nodded.

He told the others he remembered reading about Yu Chin San in the newspaper.

"Recently, Yu got elected to be the president of the Anti-Communist League for Korean Youth," Mr. Kim said, adding, "Too bad he lost the election last May."

Lady Cha said, "He was running against the most famous person in the country, Tae Jung Shin."

"Yeah," Mr. Kim said. "She was educated in America and the only female congressional candidate in the whole country."

"Tae Jung Shin was too strong an opponent for him to beat," Lady Cha said. "She also had the unlimited support of President Rhee Seung Mahn."

Mr. Kim had been impressed with Yu Chin San. Among other things, he said, "Yu opposed the incompetent, authoritarian, and cliquish Rhee Seung Mahn government."

The introductions helped the group relax a bit. Knowing where everyone was from made the people more comfortable together.

"I hope we are on the South Korean government side," Lady Cha said, referring to Republic of Korea. She let out a sigh. "I don't think the Communists made it this far, up to the top of this mountain, anyway, do you all agree?"

Everyone nodded.

That night, Hyun Jung learned that Mr. Kim was a high-ranking government official in the Department of Foreign Affairs; Lady Cha was the wife of a congressman from Andong; Moon was a professor at Hyundai University in Seoul; and the youngest among the four, Song, was a student at Myung Dong University, also in Seoul.

It was a good thing they took off from Seoul when they did. Each of them in the group would be in danger if spotted by the Northern invaders. They certainly would be regarded as enemies of the people by the Communists and would be punished (or even killed). Anyone who had achieved a certain amount of success in the South Korean society could be accused of being enemies of people. They would be shamed and ridiculed in front of masses, or even shot in public.

16

Bahdook Players

On the top of the towering mountain, a bright July morning sun woke the nine tired refugees early. No one thought about food or the fact they had spent the night in a mountaintop barley field. They started walking as soon as everyone got ready. This was what they had been doing since they left Seoul. Avoiding the battlegrounds was the only thing on everyone's mind. It was not an easy thing to hope for, when they heard the continual sound of artillery and gunshots. The fighting appeared to be going on all around them.

As they had done since they left Seoul, everyone in the group walked quietly between the barley fields and along the narrow, winding, and irregular rice terraces. Everyone was determined to walk all day, if needed. They knew they may have to walk many days to reach the South Korean government, wherever it might be.

Mr. Kim was glad the group appeared to be getting along and helped each other, like yesterday, when they crossed the swiftly-moving river and climbing up the tall mountain.

Song gave Hyun Jung a lot of attention. Sometimes, she was teased, "Song likes Hyun Jung," which made her a bit embarrassed, but she didn't really mind. Song Jung Sik liked her because he knew she liked him too. To her, he was mature, like her own brother,

Joong Yul, who she hadn't seen for almost a year now. He was a Captain in the Republic of Korea Army. Last time she heard about him, he was directing battles at the foothills of Ji Ri Mountain in the southernmost part of South Korea. He had been assigned there to lead soldiers against the Communist guerillas hiding in tunnels by Ji Ri Mountain.

"We made it this far," Keum Ja said, nodding her head. "Hopefully, we won't see any fighting."

"Yeah, we were meant to survive, I guess," Yung Hee said. "Which side do you think we are on, anyway?"

Hyun Jung noticed Yung Hee's face had gotten even darker from all the sun since leaving Seoul.

"Let's ask Mr. Kim," Lady Cha said, adjusting her brown rimmed glasses, and walked over to the leader. "Which side are we on?"

He rubbed his head, paused to think, and then whispered, "I am not certain, but I think we are on the South Korean side."

Bending her waist, Bae Jung Ja, the tall, skinny eleventh grader, whispered, "It feels different, doesn't it?"

"I know," Joo Sill agreed. "It feels somewhat easy and relaxed."

Hyun Jung didn't make any comments but listened as the upperclassmen and grown-ups talked.

"Look, down there, down there," Song cried out, pointing below to Lady Cha, who happened to be walking next to him. "Do you see down there?"

"Yeah," Lady Cha said, stretching her eyes. "*Bahdook*" (a checker game). She was taken aback.

"We are on the South side," Moon said, rolling his eyes.

After walking till late afternoon, they arrived in a small town, where many farmhouses had thatched rooves and gourd vines growing on top of the homes. The group came upon two old men, both in traditional white linen garments, Korean jacket and pants; they were leisurely playing the bahdook. Each had a male servant. Among other chores, the male servants' duties were to fanning the old men to keep them cool while they concentrated on their next move on the bahdook board.

The players didn't seem to be bothered by the travelers. They just continued with their game, even when Mr. Kim stepped closer to the two old men to confirm what they were doing. They wouldn't be distracted.

Only the men from the leisure class in South Korea could afford to take the time to play bahdook, the board game of black and white stones. One of the servants briefly glanced at Mr. Kim, but the players themselves were not distracted at all. They wouldn't let anyone else get their attention. To these two bahdook players, the travelers were like an inconvenient breeze that would soon pass.

The nine refugees from Seoul, however, had no choice but to continue walking. Their only hope was to meet up with the South Korean government and save their lives from the ever southward spreading Communist invaders.

"How much farther do you think we have to walk?" Lady Cha asked Mr. Kim. "You seem to be thinking so hard about something."

He was caught off guard by the question. He had been speechless ever since passing the two bahdook players. He was amazed to see them sit under a shade tree, leisurely playing the old game while their servants fanned them.

"Just wondering," he answered and then continued, "I thought Korea was small enough for people to get the news instantly when things happen in Seoul, but those two we just saw didn't appear to know what's been happening up North."

Walking just a couple of feet behind, Hyun Jung saw and heard the elders' comments.

"I have been thinking about that too," Lady Cha said.

"Here we are, and all the refugees on the highway, scared and running for their lives, and those two old men have nothing to do but play bahdook under a shade tree while their servants fan them?"

Mr. Kim shook his head, though gently. Walking just a couple of feet behind, Hyun Jung saw and heard the elders' comments.

"What's the next town, do you know?" Lady Cha asked Mr. Kim. "Do you have any idea?"

"Let's see," he said.

"I say, stay in the backcountry," Joo Sill said. "We cannot take any chances."

"Yes, we still have to be careful with what we say," Mr. Kim said. "We can't know who they are, and which side they are on."

"That's the tough part," Lady Cha said, while attempting to keep up with the leader.

"I agree it's better to avoid the main highway," Moon said. "It's too jammed with refugees. We could all step on each other's toes, so close. Let me go ahead. There is one other road we can take"

Song said to Moon, "I will join you, please take me along."

Hyun Jung quietly noticed Song agreeing with Moon.

After walking for a while, Song and Moon passed the grown-ups and continued ahead.

"Don't get too far ahead," Mr. Kim hollered at the two younger men.

The grown-ups were exhausted. They had no choice, however, but to walk, walk, and walk, and keep heading toward the south to meet up with their retreating government.

The group was taken aback when they saw Moon and Song rushing back toward them.

"Take your time, and say what you want to say," Mr. Kim told Moon and Song, who appeared anxious to say something.

"We found a nice little river," Moon said, stepping closer to the leader. He repeated what he had just told the rest of the group. "We found a perfect spot for tonight."

Lady Cha and the five Ewha girls looked puzzled.

"It's getting dark," Song said. "We might just spend the night there tonight, by the river, and have a good night's rest, then start early tomorrow. It's not too far."

"Not a bad idea," Mr. Kim said, looking at Lady Cha.

She nodded, and they all continued down the trail.

17

Fifteen Men from Geum San

The small stream looked inviting to the fleeing men. Perhaps they could take a little break for the night. Fifteen men from Geum San stopped for the night by the highway that led to Daegu. They had walked all day and had enough of walking.

"It's better to rest here tonight and take off early tomorrow morning," said Kwon, the eldest in the group. "My legs are killing me, Aigoo, aigoo… My legs."

A few feet down from the only highway in the country, the men found a spot to rest for the night.

"I'm starving," Lee said. "We haven't had any food since last night."

"Who has the bag with rice balls?" Park, the leader, asked. "Bring the bag and let's eat."

Some of the men looked around, looking for something that resembled water to help wash down the now hardened rice balls.

"You just have to walk down there," Kwon said, pointing to the small stream below. "Cup your hands scoop some of the water up, and drink. Hurry, go, get some. Let me know how it is."

"That stream, sir?" Lee asked, looking at the murky stream below.

"We don't have any choice," Kwon said.

"The rice won't go down our throats without something wet," Lee said, peeling the wraps from a small bag of kimchi.

"Any chopsticks?" Park asked.

"Oh, who needs chopsticks during wartime?" Kwon exclaimed, looking for some branches from nearby shrub. "Cut some of these branches and make chopsticks, if you really must have chopsticks."

Byun rushed down to the murky stream. When he got there, he kneeled down, scooped up some water with his cupped hand, and drank it. Kwon and Lee followed Byun.

The next morning, the fifteen men woke up before dawn and began walking south, toward Daegu, where the South Korean government was supposed to have settled.

"The road is packed," Kwon said, plopping down under a roadside tree. Park joined him, wiping the sweat from his forehead with his handkerchief. "We won't get there until late afternoon, at the earliest."

"I hope we get there before dark," Lee said.

"We supported her," Park said, shaking his head. "She just disappeared, without a word to us." He shook his head.

"I know," Kwon said. "What did I tell you? She left us just to save her own neck. We went too far for her. We didn't have to criticize her opponent so severely."

"Yu Chin San wasn't as bad as we painted him to be," Byun said.

"However, it's water under the bridge. All done. It's in the past," Park said, shaking his head.

"The thing is," Kwon said, shaking his head, "we don't know a soul in Daegu."

Lee nodded. "She looked so good. Such an attractive candidate. She was the only woman in the whole country running for congress. Her American education and backing of the old man, Rhee Seung Mahn, was so attractive, then."

"We shouldn't have supported that woman," Kwon said, slowly shaking his small, bald head.

"I wasn't totally happy going with her, but she had the backing of President Rhee, and all that," Park continued. "Could almost taste how wonderful things would be when we just got her elected."

"I guess she really didn't care about us, or anyone else, but her own neck," Byun said. "That's why we shouldn't have trusted a woman."

The national election had been held on May 10, just one month or so ago. It had gotten a lot of attention. The only woman in the country running for congress opposed Yu Chin San, an independent who was adamantly against the policies of the president. Although the election was in a provincial district, Geum San, it was regarded as so important that the results had been reported from the rooftop of the City Hall of Seoul for twenty-four hours a day, with red and green neon signs.

"No choice," Kwon said. "We have to find Yu Chin San. I think he took off from Daejun and is already in Daegu, I am pretty sure."

"How can we do that?" Park snapped. "We tried so hard to smear his reputation."

Everyone nodded.

"Actually, we did too much," Park continued. "Made Yu look like anything but what he really was, a decent man and a patriot. I know when he practiced law, he took a lot of Korean political prisoners out of Japanese jails." Park was referring to Yu Chin San's patriotic activity during the Japanese occupation of Korea from 1910 to 1945. He continued, "I know that much."

"He fought the Japs and worked for the Korean government in exile in China," Kwon continued. "More specifically, he was in Shanghai and later in Chong Ch'ing, you know."

The group became quiet. No one could imagine how they'd survive when they got to Daegu; together with Busan, they were the only two big cities still left in South Korea.

"Well, now what?" Park said. "What can we do when we get to Daegu? We cannot even find one room for us fifteen to squeeze in, not to mention lying down and stretching our tired legs at night."

The fifteen men sat quietly with their eyes cast down.

"We just have to find Yu Chin San when we get to Daegu. Forget things like pride," Lee said. "He is the only person we know who would know people in high enough place in South Korean government to help us."

"But Yu is not in the government," Kwon said.

"Doesn't matter," Park replied. "He knows more people in high government positions than we do. All he can do is tell us to get lost."

"That's right," Byun said. "He is our only hope."

"But how?" Kwon asked.

"When we get there, we will check and see where he stays," Park said, looking at Kwon.

"But there are so many refugees all over the city, I am sure," Lee said.

"It's not the time to worry about the past or humiliation. None of that will bring us a spot to lay our tired bodies down to rest tonight," Park said, shaking his head.

Kwon said, "When we get to Daegu, Park and I will first go to the City Hall. They should know where the South Korean government people are."

No one talked. They all kept their heads down and waited.

"We cannot be too choosey," Park mumbled. "What is pride?"

18

Walking through a Burning City

The sky was pitch-black, not even a slight sign of light anywhere. All nine of the refugees from Seoul huddled together while walking behind their leader, Mr. Kim. The whole world appeared to have turned into one dark tunnel.

"Let's just stay close together," Mr. Kim said. He added, "We'll see what comes next." He turned to Hyun Jung and asked, "All right back there, kkoma?"

"Yes," she answered, tightening her lips. She liked getting his attention and felt safer knowing the leader was thinking about her.

They walked for a while without saying anything to each other, just putting one foot ahead of the other, as they had been doing since they left Seoul three days before. All were hoping they would meet up with their government sooner rather than later.

Hyun Jung overheard the leader say to Lady Cha, in a hushed voice, "Isn't that Chung Joo?" It was the capital of North Choong Chung Do.

Lady Cha waited awhile and then said, "Yeah, I think so, but I am not too sure." She dropped her voice and then whispered, "Looks like it's on fire."

"Oh, good," Kim Keum Ja said, looking straight ahead. "At least now we can see the road."

Moon and Song stepped back to the group to make sure everything was alright with everyone to go ahead toward Chung Joo.

"I think so, too," Joo Sill said. "Oh, I feel some breeze."

The group came closer and waited for the leader to speak. "We have no choice but to walk through the city," Mr. Kim said, looking at the city ahead.

"There are no other roads to take," Song agreed.

As they walked closer to Chung Joo, Hyun Jung saw different shades of colors: orange, deep red, black, burnt umber, charcoal, smoked gray, streaks of light red flames, and even white. As they walked closer, at one point, she saw dark orange whirling up to the sky. They continued without any further words. Hyun Jung lifted her bent arm to shield her face as she saw a bright orange, yellow and black flame rushing toward her. She quickly covered her eyes with her two hands.

The flame lit up the world. What a frightening change from the darkness they had endured just a minute ago. Hyun Jung saw the night sky lit up like a red dome in flame, so bright and glowing with streaks of dark lines here and there. She was frightened to go forward. As the group inched closer, they slowed down. Everyone looked with dread toward the burning red flames.

Finally, Mr. Kim repeated, "We have no choice, because there is no other road." Everybody was silent. He added, "We must walk through it, somehow, and make it."

"Just walk fast," Moon said.

Mr. Kim stopped, turned around, and counted heads again. He wanted to make sure all nine in his group were there with him. They were.

Though less packed than the main highway, the road to Chung Joo had a lot of refugees.

Yung Hee came to Hyun Jung and asked quietly, "Tired?" Hyun Jung shook her head and answered, "No."

"You think you can keep up with the group?"

Hyun Jung nodded and said, "Yes, of course." The thirteen-year-old sucked in her answer and walked right behind her fellowship sister, Yung Hee.

Soon afterwards, Joo Sill came over to Hyun Jung and said, "I'm glad you are not holding us back. You didn't even cry once."

"Of course not," Yung Hee said, rather curtly. Hyun Jung's mind wasn't peaceful; in fact, she was scared about walking through the burning city, but she wouldn't show it.

"She is doing fine," Mr. Kim said. "Here, kkoma, get close to me. I will go first, and then you walk right behind me, okay?"

They continued through the burning city; the air felt heavy and hot. The ground was too hot. It felt like being inside of a burning tunnel. Hyun Jung stepped right behind the leader and continued walking. She remembered her promise not to cry and become a hindrance to the group. Even though the bottoms of her feet felt too hot to walk, she didn't let anyone know about it. She decided not to think about the burning heat on the bottoms of her feet. She continued taking big steps, while looking all around and watching where she was stepping; down the narrow passageway to her left, Hyun Jung glimpsed a thatched roof that was on fire; it was held up by a tattered and ragged mud wall. The thatched roof had caught on fire, and chunks of burning straw mixed into mud, dropping to the ground.

She heard Mr. Kim shouting, "Don't look," but it was too late.

At that very moment, Hyun Jung happened to look to her left. She quickly turned her head back, but not before she saw a dead man; his arms were sizzling. His round bare head rested on his two folded arms on top of his bent legs. She quickly turned away. Both his feet were on the ground, squatting, but his bare shoulder was sizzling like meat on a skewer.

"Don't turn, just look ahead," Mr. Kim commanded again, but it was too late. Hyun Jung had already seen it. *He must have tried to fight off the flame from his face,* Hyun Jung thought. *But finally surrendered to the hot burning flame. Poor thing.*

"Don't look," the leader said. "Just keep walking forward, continue. Walk."

But Hyun Jung gave another quick glance at the sizzling man. Just then, Song, who had been walking in the back of the group, shouted loudly, "Look out! Step back!" She quickly looked up and saw a burning telephone pole that was about to fall down right in front of the group. Everyone stopped walking; they waited for a moment and then edged back, barely avoiding the glowing giant pole as it struck the ground near them. Flaming balls of fire fell here and there like sparks from an active volcano.

"Oh," Hyun Jung groaned loudly, reaching for her foot. The bottoms of her feet were too hot to walk.

"Just endure for a few more minutes, kkoma, will you?" Mr. Kim pleaded. "We are almost in a safe place."

At last, finally, they made it through the burning city. When everyone had emerged from Chung Joo, Mr. Kim gathered up his group to make sure everyone was there. Hyun Jung could feel the muggy and smoky hot air still clinging to her.

"We've passed the burning city," Mr. Kim said. "We all made it."

"That's the most important thing of all," Lady Cha said. "Everyone is here. God looks out for us."

After they passed through Chung Joo, the road ahead suddenly turned dark again. It got even darker the farther they looked. As they walked away from the burning city, the world turned pitch-black.

"Come closer, everyone," Mr. Kim said.

19

Fifteen Men from Geum San

Kwon began handing out the small rice balls and told the hungry men, "Here, we can only have one each and no more."

The air was chilly for a July morning. For the fifteen men fleeing from Geum San, it was very special day. Each of the men had been born and grew up in that community. In fact, it was their first night away since they left their home and family.

Kwon yawned, stretching his arms above his head. He then brusquely rubbed his bald head to wake himself up. They were still at the roadside where they had slept the night before. This was the only highway in all of Korea. The road led to the south and eventually to Daegu, where the South Korean government supposedly had taken refuge.

Byun took a bite of the rice ball, shook his head, and spit it out. "Aigoo."

"What's the matter?" Lee asked.

"Too dry," Byun continued. "Cannot eat this dry *bahp* [cooked rice] without something to wash it down with."

"Go down there," Kwon said, pointing to the small muddy pond below the road. "You might find some water down there."

"What can I use to scoop it up?" Byun asked back.

"What do you think?" Park asked. "Just like before, use your hands. We have to use everything we have. It's wartime."

"I will go down with you," Lee said, leaping up from his seat. The two youngest in the group stepped down to get some water, and a half dozen men followed.

"Cup your hands and scoop some up," Kwon hollered.

No one talked. They knew too well that talking wouldn't do any good. Still, they couldn't help but wondering why the old man, President Rhee Seung Mahn, was so inept as not to know what was going on. How could he surrender the capital city to the bbahl-gehng-ee?

"Here, try this," Kwon said to Park, looking around first before handing over the small jug. He had just taken a swallow for himself and continued, "Look at the road; people are all over already this morning. Water, or no water, we need to hurry; it will still take a good whole day to Daegu, you know."

Byun and Lee climbed back up with a bit more satisfied look.

"So how was the water down there? Did you drink it?" Park asked the two young men.

"Well, sir," Lee answered, jerking up his shoulders. "It wasn't too bad; still water."

"Bahp is easier to swallow with some water, all in all," Byun said.

"Oh, my back," Park said, wrinkling his forehead.

"Move your body left to right, like this," Lee said, gazing at the endless line of refugees on the highway.

"These people must not have slept," Kwon said. "The road is already packed. I guess they are all going to Daegu."

"Sleeping on this hard rock isn't easy," Park complained.

"Nothing's going to be easy from this point on. We will be lucky to be alive," Kwon said.

At that moment, a strange man walked over and, without hesitation, asked, "Do you have a cigarette?" The man continued, "Just for one puff?"

"We don't have any," Park said. "Please go back." His stern tone of voice chased the man away; he disappeared quickly into the line of refugees.

"What did he want?" Kwon asked.

"A cigarette," Park said, shaking his head slightly. "Nothing to worry about."

"One never knows," Kwon said.

"Seriously, where can we go when we get to Daegu?" Lee asked, lightly scratching his head. "We don't know anybody there."

"We will just have to look up Yu Chin San," Kwon said, after taking a sip of his water. "He can just say, 'Don't bother me,' and turn us away."

"Now, we know," Byun said.

"We didn't have to be so hard on him," Kwon said. "To get him defeated, a fine man, actually."

No one spoke; each man kept quiet and stared down at the ground.

"Who'd have known that the world would turn upside down like this, practically overnight?" Park said, shaking his head.

Even though these men were prominent individuals in Geum San, they would be nobody in Daegu. Their first concern would be to find a spot to sleep in.

In Daegu, a city of almost two million people, these fifteen men would be out of their element. They would be so uncomfortable there, with speaking different dialects, to mention just one, like fish out of water. Especially, they knew no one in the city.

Simply put, they had no connection in that capital city, Daegu of Kyung Sang Book Do.

The Color Red

"Light," Mr. Kim said, with a surprised tone of voice. "Do you all see the light over there?" The leader pointed ahead of everyone standing near him.

The group of nine from Seoul walked closely with their leader on the narrow rice terrace. They kept their eyes on a flickering blue light far ahead.

"It's got to be a checkpoint or something," Lady Cha whispered, turning toward Joo Sill. "I hope it's on the South Korean side."

No one answered. The group huddled close, while continuing to walk, though slowly; their steps carried them forward.

They knew that as long as they stayed close, there was a chance they would come out alive. Again, Hyun Jung was glad she and her Ewha upperclassmen had joined with these grown-ups. As the group came nearer to the flickering light, everyone paused, and they let their leader speak.

Mr. Kim focused on the far-away blue light and said, "It's a building."

They were hopeful. However, they could not be sure who was inside the building. They could be North Korean soldiers, or South Korean sympathizers.

When the group finally arrived at a makeshift large building, one by one, each person stepped up on the wobbly plywood steps that led them to the door. They all went inside through a narrow door.

Inside, Hyun Jung noticed one dim lightbulb dangling down from the tall ceiling, right in the middle of the room. The light bulb was connected to a long, skinny rope. Mr. Kim motioned for everyone to take a seat at the narrow metal bench placed up against the wall on the far-right side. The empty room was like a large cave with no sign of humanity, and everything was dark gray.

"You all wait here," Mr. Kim said, then he turned to Lady Cha and asked, "Join me?"

The two grown-ups walked across the room towards what appeared to be some offices. After checking several locked doors, they finally came to a handwritten sign that read, "Inspector and the Office of the Korean Central Intelligence Agency (KCIA)." Mr. Kim rushed back to his group and whispered, "It's a South Korean military post."

Everyone was relieved to hear that. They finally had made it to the South Korean side. Hyun Jung felt tears of relief, but she forced them away. They were finally safe, the side of the Republic of Korea, the South Korean side.

Together, the leader and Lady Cha quietly walked into the office that housed two expressionless South Korean soldiers. This room was just as dim as the large waiting hall. Inside the small office, they saw two desks and two chairs. The wall was bare. The only picture on the wall was a framed, lifeless photo of Rhee Seung Mahn, the president of the Republic of Korea, the man who lost the capital city to the Communist regime. The picture was hanging slightly crooked.

Mr. Kim greeted the two South Korean uniformed soldiers, Lieutenant Lee and his assistant, Sergeant Koo.

They told Mr. Kim and Lady Cha to empty their pockets and open the little bags they had been carrying with them since Seoul.

"Passed," the Lieutenant announced after Lady Cha and Mr. Kim opened their bags for inspection.

When Mr. Kim and Lady Cha stepped out of the inspector's office, the twelfth graders, Jung Joo Sill and Ko Yung Hee, went into the room to be checked. They each passed the bag search rather swiftly, also.

Next in line were the two eleventh graders: Bae Jung Ja, the taller of the two, and Kim Keum Ja, the short and chubbier one. Both girls went in and opened their bags to get inspected. When Keum Ja's bag was opened, the inspector, Lieutenant Lee, instantly frowned, bent at his waist, and looked again. He saw a square of red cloth inside Kim Keum Ja's bag.

"What's this?" Lieutenant Lee asked; his loud voice rang out beyond the inspection office and all the way over to the waiting room, where the group from Seoul were listening.

Mr. Kim leapt up, without saying a word, and then rushed back to the inspection office. When he entered the office filled with soldiers, he saw Lieutenant Lee holding a small, five-by-five-inch square of red fabric. The main thing the South Korean soldiers were looking for were any Communist spies in disguise or any signs of sympathy or loyalty toward the Communists.

The KCIA inspectors were furious. Red was the color of Communism. The soldiers believed Keum Ja could be a Communist spy, or a Communist sympathizer, or even a messenger. Anything was possible.

"What's this?" the inspector shouted at Keum Ja.

"I don't know how it got there, sir." Keum Ja sucked in, crying. The inspector, however, just got angrier.

Mr. Kim realized how serious the situation was. This was happening in a war zone.

He quickly turned to the crying, sniffling, and whimpering Keum Ja and commanded, "What are you doing? You should get down on your knees and beg for forgiveness."

Then, Kim Keum Ja immediately dropped to her knees and rubbed her hands together for forgiveness, as the leader had told her to do.

The infuriated inspector, Lieutenant Lee, however, wouldn't budge. With hands on his hips, he commanded Sergeant Koo to get rid of the whole group.

"We don't have the time to fool around with this nonsense." The Lieutenant was fuming. "Load them all up. Load them up in the truck, these troublemakers. Take them up to the mountain and finish them off."

Sergeant Koo hesitated a bit, but the Lieutenant said in a louder tone of voice, "What are you doing?" The Lieutenant couldn't be bothered with this group any longer. "We don't have all day."

Kim Keum Ja, still on her knees, covered her face with both hands and begged, "Aigoo. I am sorry. Please. Let me live!"

"How dare she, carrying the red piece cloth," the angry Lieutenant shouted, both hands still on his waist. "What's this? A kid's game? Take them away, hurry."

Mr. Kim then took Keum Ja out of the room to join the rest of the group. The group huddled around, anxious to find out what was going on.

Mr. Kim, without saying a word to anyone, rushed back into the KCIA inspector's room. He went over to the still-fuming Lieutenant and whispered in his ear, "Chairman Yu Chin San's daughter is in our group, sir."

"What?" Inspector Lee said, leaning his head toward Mr. Kim.

"She has been with us for the last ten days, sir."

At first, Lieutenant Lee looked suspiciously at Mr. Kim.

"Yes, sir."

"We don't have the time to listen to any nonsense."

"Please, sir. She has been with us since Seoul, sir." He was insistent and pleaded, looking directly into the Lieutenant's eyes.

The phone rang.

"Major Choi," Lieutenant Lee said into the phone. "Yes, sir."

It was the chief of the KCIA, the top officer of South Korea's Eastern Region, Lieutenant Lee's boss.

Since the war broke out, the Eastern Region had become quite important as the Busan Perimeter to the South Korean people, who were now helplessly fleeing southward as city after city fell into the hands of the Communists.

"Yes, sir … rather routine, sir … from Seoul … but we found a scrap of red cloth in one of the girl student's bag, sir. … Other than that …"

"What?" The Major said. "How old is the girl?" His voice could be heard even in the other room.

"Well, sir." The Lieutenant put his hand on the phone to cover the speaker, then turned his head towards Mr. Kim, who had been standing by, and asked, "How old is the student?"

"Eleventh grader, sir," he answered.

The Lieutenant repeated what the leader said into the phone, "Eleventh grader, sir."

"Be thorough, understand? Troublemakers, these bbahl-gehng-ee."

"Yes, sir," Lieutenant Lee said into the phone. "Oh, sir, among them, sir, Chairman Yu Chin San's daughter is in the group, sir."

"What?" Major Choi said. "Wait a minute. Hold everything until I get there, understand?"

"Yes, sir."

The Major hung up the phone. Then, a few minutes later, he called back and told the Lieutenant, "Let the rest of the people go on their own ways. I will handle it when I get there. Keep Chairman Yu Chin San's daughter until I get there, understand?"

Before Hyun Jung could realize what was happening, Mr. Kim's original group, Lady Cha and the three men, went to Andong, their original destination. Joo Sill continued on to Busan. Yung Hee went with Joo Sill because the Communists had already taken her hometown in Kang Won Do. Bae Jung Ja and Kim Keum Ja also joined Joo Sill, for South Chula Do, their hometown, was saturated with newly emboldened Communist guerillas from nearby Ji Ri Mountain. Everybody could envision how the bbahl-gehng-ee would raise havoc in their hometown.

Everybody, except Hyun Jung, now left the checkpoint and began walking toward Busan, Joo Sill's hometown and the southernmost port city in Korea.

Alone in the cave-like waiting room, Hyun Jung quietly sat on the metal bench and waited for Major Choi to show up, as she was told to do by Lieutenant Lee.

Almost ten minutes passed, when Hyun Jung noticed Lieutenant Lee walking toward her. When he got closer, he said, "Major Choi wants to see you. He just left Daegu."

The Lieutenant continued, "He just left Daegu. All your friends left for their own homes. It won't be long before the Major gets here. He is on his way here. Want anything to drink?"

Hyun Jung shook her head and said, "No."

Hyun Jung was sad that the others in her group had already taken off. She didn't even get to say good-bye to them. At the same time, she was glad their lives had been spared and they would be reuniting with their families. *Things could have been worse*, she thought.

Now, the once-empty waiting room was filled with a fresh flock of refugees.

"Next," a soldier called out. A large group, more than ten, went together into the inspection room to prove they were not on the side of Communist invaders. That large group left the inspector's office rather swiftly.

The waiting room was empty once again. Hyun Jung still sat there, waiting for the Major to show up, as she was told to do. She sat on the same bench, and on the same spot, and alone.

21

Pesky Little Girl

Now that Hyun Jung was in the South Korean side, she was relieved. She had some time to herself, instead of running to save her life from the invaders. She hadn't heard from her family for over two months now. In May, before the war broke out, her mother had to go down to Jin San to attend to the aftermath of the election. But now, Hyun Jung had no idea where her mother was. As far as she was concerned, her whole family was in danger from the Communist invaders and from the guerillas. Ji Ri Mountain, near her hometown, Jin San, was well known for troublemakers.

As Hyun Jung sat in the dark hall of the checkpoint to wait for Major Choi, her mind wandered. She heard her mother's soft voice: *My daughter was born with a thousand lucks.* She was grateful that her mother was so good to her. As her mother had said, deep down, she herself believed she was a lucky person to have such a kindhearted mother. Hyun Jung remembered one day, her mother, wearing a *jugori,* a soft yellow white traditional Korean top, and white long *chima* (skirt), said with a loving voice, "You were born with a thousand lucks." She missed seeing the loving expression on her mother's face.

While her thoughts wandered, she noticed a short, skinny guy looking her way from across the hall. He was wearing an army uniform with a cap that was too large for his pointed, boney narrow face. Hyun Jung quickly lowered her eyes when she spotted a gun hanging down from the guy's shoulder.

He gestured for her to come towards him, but Hyun Jung quickly turned her head away and pretended not to see. She decided to just ignore him. However, a few minutes later, the guy with the skinny face came over to her.

He stood close to her and asked, "Want anything?"

Clenching her little bag closer to her bosom, she shook her head and said, "No."

"All your friends went their own ways."

"Yes?" Hyun Jung asked and quickly turned her eyes away from him.

"We freed them, let them go," he continued. "Everybody in your group went to their own homes, I guess."

"I know," Hyun Jung said. "Lieutenant Lee told me."

She was relieved they were let go instead of taken up to the mountaintop to be "finished," as the angry officer had commanded when he saw the piece of red cloth in Kim Keum Ja's bag.

"You will have to wait for a while," the guy said. "Want something to drink or something to eat?"

Hyun Jung shook her head.

"I will send someone over to take you; wait right there."

"No, I am okay, really."

Hyun Jung was glad to see him walking away.

Like a pesky nuisance, however, the short guy reappeared. He came toward Hyun Jung again and said, "Let's go and get something to drink."

"I'm okay," Hyun Jung said into her bosom, shaking her head left to right.

"Lieutenant Lee told me to take you to the store up the hill and get you something to drink."

It was dark outside. He led her into a narrow passageway at the side of the large checkpoint building. She realized she had better collect her thoughts and remembered a Korean saying, *Must think clearly even while being dragged away by a tiger.*

They walked around the building. Hyun Jung watched him step into a narrow passageway.

"Just follow me," he said.

She held her breath and shook her head.

"No," she protested. "Too dark. I am going back inside." *There's something about this guy I cannot trust,* she thought.

He was walking toward bushes, away from the building. She held herself very still and let him get ahead. Suddenly, she felt everything was darker, quieter, and very still. She was thinking how she could escape.

"I told you to just follow me," he said. "Do as I say."

"Where are we?"

"You are a pesky little girl."

"It's too dark," Hyun Jung said. "I want to go back to the checkpoint."

When she hesitated, he grabbed her away from the passageway and pulled her into what felt like an overgrown bush. He was forceful. He pulled her in with all his might. She couldn't resist him. He knew his way, but she didn't. Before she could pull away, he pushed her down on the ground.

He covered her mouth with his hand and whispered, "Don't make any sound."

She tried to push him away with all the strength she could muster.

"Don't do anything foolish," he commanded. "Just do as I say."

She felt his rigid body on top of her. She struggled to push him off of her, but his grip on her was too tight. They struggled as he tried to take control of her body, while she tried to push him off. He got on top of her and searched for her lips. Trying to avoid his mouth, she turned her head this way and that. Finally, she felt his tongue in her mouth. At that very moment, she gathered her strength and then bit his tongue, with all the strength she could muster.

He screamed in pain and rolled off of her. "Ow, you little bit—"

She jumped up, grabbed her little bag, and began running away from the guy. She could hear him nursing his wounds while making animal sounds. "You little … ou …" He held his mouth with his both hands and squatted down. She could imagine all that, even in the dark.

Hyun Jung wasn't sure just where she was. She crouched quietly behind a bush and sat very still, listening, but not making any sound. She held her breath. The world got so still and quiet. She thought she heard something rustling and waited without making any sound, whatsoever.

Still behind the bush, she quietly adjusted her clothes, picked up her little bag, and began crawling away from that bony little guy. She crawled to her left, watching the spot where the guy had been, hoping it would be the way back to the checkpoint, but she didn't see the building. She tried to be alert about her situation and make sense of where she was in relation to the checkpoint. But it was no use. The night was too dark. As her despair grew, she happened to turn to her left and spotted a dim light far away.

Hyun Jung paused and listened, but the whole world was too quiet, deadly quiet. She wanted to make sure she was taking the right direction back to the checkpoint. She got on her knees first then moved into a squatting position and began inching, slowly, towards the light.

Frightened, Hyun Jung tried to quiet down her thumping heart by placing her hand on it and listening attentively. Finally, after helpless struggle and search, she approached the dim light. After looking around to make sure the guy wasn't close by, still on her knees, she crawled forward. Stopping every few minutes, the thirteen-year-old checked around and listened before resuming, inching toward the dim light.

When she stepped into the checkpoint building, she felt as though she was coming back to a place of refuge and warmth. However, when she looked around, she noticed it was still empty. Nothing had changed. Not a person was in sight. It was quiet, eerily quiet. She held her little bag even tighter and kept her eyes searching for any sign of movement, looking left and right.

Finally, she found the same bench where she had been sitting, waiting for the Major to show up, as Lieutenant Lee told her. Yu Hyun Jung from Jin San and Ewha Girl's Middle School in Seoul tried to calm herself as though nothing had happened to her in this war-ravaged mountainside military checkpoint.

22

"Whole Country Is Running Away"

Hyun Jung was too proud to show how frightened she really felt. How humiliating it would be to let them know the little guy with the pointed face tried to take advantage of her. She wouldn't let that happen. *Even though I'm all alone in this battlefield checkpoint, nobody will take advantage of me,* she told to herself. She might seem like an orphan right now, in this wartime, but she would never forget who she really was: a girl from an important Yu family in South Choong Chung Do—Yu Chin San's daughter.

Hyun Jung sat on the same bench where she had been told to wait for the Major. After a brief moment, she became disoriented and forgot why she was sitting all by herself, in this empty, dark place, with only a lightbulb dangling down from the ceiling in the middle of this large barn-like place.

Finally, Lieutenant Lee appeared in front of Hyun Jung and said, "It won't be long, about ten or fifteen more minutes." Hyun Jung quietly nodded. "They are all gone now. You saw all those people, didn't you, a few minutes ago?"

She didn't respond.

The Lieutenant continued, "Looks like the whole country is running away. We too? Who knows?" The Lieutenant said all these things to himself, shrugging his shoulders. He then remarked, "You have been very patient. It won't be long." He walked back to his office.

Hyun Jung clutched her little bag, glancing at the door to see who might be entering. Just then, a string of refugees poured into the room. Among them were a very old gray-haired Halmuhni, a stout middle-aged man, a middle-aged woman, and two boys. Neither of the boys looked to be older than ten.

The man walked over to Hyun Jung and asked, "Where's the office?"

She directed him to the room and moved over to offer the Halmuhni a seat on the bench. She then rose from the bench so the whole family could sit together. Looking at their rumpled clothes and messed-up hair, she could see that they, too, had been walking for days.

They whispered to each other in low voices, like people do when they don't know whether they are still in the Communist side, or on the South Korean side. "I'll be right back," the man said to his group and then walked to the office.

"Student," the middle-aged woman asked Hyun Jung, "where are you from?"

"Seoul, ma'am."

"Seoul is already taken over by them; is that why you left?"

Hyun Jung didn't answer. Instead, she lowered her head without a word.

"When did you leave Seoul?" the woman asked.

"Ten days ago, ma'am."

"Alone?" the lady continued, "Aigoo," then she asked, "Alone?"

"With my *sunbae unees* (upper classmates), ma'am."

The man came out of the inspection office with a grin on his copper-brown face and whispered, "It's the South side, our side."

"Oh," the Halmuhni said quietly, letting out a sigh.

The man then said, "They want us to come in to have our bags checked."

"We have nothing, just empty hands," the middle-aged woman said, getting up from the bench.

"They want to make sure we are not carrying anything to help the enemies," the man continued. "Don't worry, just go in and do whatever the officers tell you to do."

Everyone in the group got up and headed for the inspection office.

As soon as the group left, another large group of people stepped into this once-empty checkpoint building. With their messed-up clothes and hair, they also looked as though they had been walking for days. *Maybe they are refugees from Seoul, like I am,* Hyun Jung thought, as she continued to wait for the Major to arrive.

23

Major Choi

As soon as he stepped into the checkpoint, before even going over to his office, Major Choi went into the room to meet Hyun Jung. She had been waiting for him to arrive for hours.

He knew the young girl in a school uniform of white blouse and dark skirt was Yu Chin San's daughter. Lieutenant Lee had described her accurately when they talked over the phone.

Looking at Hyun Jung, the Major said, "You have your father's eyes, with double folds."

Hyun Jung wasn't too surprised to hear this comment because these types of remarks about one's looks were frequently made by Korean people when meeting a person for the first time.

Hyun Jung stood up and bowed to Major Choi, the KCIA chief of Pohang Perimeter in the Eastern Region. He was tall and large, with broad shoulders and a husky, booming voice. His pockmarked face was on the dark side, even for a Korean man.

"It's okay," the Major said. "Sit down, sit down. You must be tired."

Then, he rushed off to his office, where Lieutenant Lee and Sergeant Koo were expecting him. When they saw their boss, the two soldiers leaped up and saluted the Major.

"Have the girl student come in," Major Choi told Lieutenant Lee, who told the sergeant to bring Hyun Jung into the office.

While they waited, Major Choi told Lieutenant Lee to sit in the chair in front of him. He then started to tell him about Hyun Jung's father. "Yu Chin San was one man in Korean politics I admire. I liked that Yu Chin San was the first president of the League of Anti-Communism for Korean Youth."

"Yes, sir."

"Another thing I liked about him was that he opposed Rhee Seung Mahn, the inept old man," he said, glancing at the photo of the country's president on the wall. "How could he lose our capital city to bbahl-gehng-ee?"

For a brief moment, the Major thought about how wonderful it would be if he could actually meet Yu Chin San. How fortunate and honored that he was taking Yu's daughter to his own home. It could possibly mean opening doors to the tightly knit Korean hierarchical society, the largely Confucianism-influenced yangban class. It might even help him when he was ready to go up for a promotion. He may go up for a position as General, someday. Major Choi knew Yu occupied an influential position in Korean politics.

Holding her little bag up against her bosom, Hyun Jung followed Sergeant Koo into the Major's office.

"Have a seat, have a seat," the Major said to Hyun Jung, pointing to a chair in front of his large desk. He knew her father, Yu Chin San, was a patriot who loved his country and was strongly against Communism. This much he knew about the father of the young girl student sitting in front of him. "So how long have you been walking?" he asked.

"Since the fifth of July, sir."

Lieutenant Lee said, "I need to help Sergeant Koo, sir."

"Okay, you are dismissed," the Major responded, nodding to the Lieutenant, and then he resumed talking to Hyun Jung. "Wait a minute, today is July 15, that means you have been walking for ten days?"

"Yes, sir."

"How did that happen?" he asked, searching Hyun Jung's eyes. "Where was your family?"

"Well, sir," she began, "I live on my school campus, sir."

"Oh? Why?"

"My father was afraid of the Seoul traffic, sir."

"I know something about the traffic in Seoul; it can be bad."

"My father says we can't depend on machines; they can break down. He used to say to me, 'A car is a machine; if it breaks down, how can you make to your class?'"

"I see," the Major said. "So …?"

"On the day when Seoul was taken," Hyun Jung said, "no one came to pick me up at my school."

"Really? Why not?"

"Well, my whole family went to Jin San, sir," she explained, "for the election, last month, sir."

"Oh, yes, I know, I know all about that."

"See, my father ran for the Parliament but lost to Congresswoman Tae Jung Shin, sir."

"I know, I know," Major Choi said, nodding his head. "I have been following that election; your father should have won that one." He continued, "I will find him for you. Your father is a great man." Hyun Jung nodded, and the Major added, "You are going home with me."

"Yes?"

"I will find your father for you. Do not worry. I will find him for you."

"Thank you."

"I promise," the Major said. "Right now, the South Korean government is in Daegu. The Communists are too strong, and our government is busy losing the war. We get pushed down, down, and down."

Hyun Jung did not reply.

"I live in Pohang with my family. You'll like my two children, Soon Hee and Soon Tae. Soon Hee is a little younger than you." The Major looked closely at Hyun Jung. "How old are you?"

"Thirteen, sir."

"Soon Hee is eleven, and Soon Tae is nine; they are good kids, and you will like their mother, too. You can live at my house until I find your father."

"Thank you, sir." She was grateful to Major Choi. *How kind of him to want to help me out,* she thought.

He resumed talking again. "Let me see. I never met your father, but I have seen his pictures in newspapers. As I already have said, you resemble your father, with a pair of big eyes and double-folded eyelids."

Again, Hyun Jung wasn't surprised at the comment. She had heard the same comment before from other grown-ups when she first met them. Each time, she accepted the comment with silence.

The Major said, "So you were in Seoul when the Communists came in?"

"Yes, sir. We left Seoul on July 5, sir."

"So you were in Seoul when the Communists invaded the capital city?" he asked again.

"Yes, sir," Hyun Jung said quietly.

The Major shook his head and then asked, "What happened next?"

"The Communist soldiers came to our dorm and took all our rice, sir." The Major listened without comment. "That's when our school principal, Principal Jo, told us to leave, sir."

"Is that right? That's terrible."

"Principal Jo said, 'We don't have any rice to feed you.' Then he gave some money to an upperclassman, Jung Joo Sill, and told her to take a few more girls and leave."

24

The News from Seoul

Sitting back in his desk chair, Major Choi remembered seeing some of the pictures of Yu Chin San, the father of the girl student who was sitting in front of him. In fact, he had seen many pictures of Yu Chin San in newspapers, booklets, and so on. One of his distinguishing features was the manicured mustache on his slim face. In addition, he had large eyes with double folds and wavy black hair. Those features weren't very common among Korean men.

"Your family," the Major said. "Are they still in Geum San?"

"Jin San, sir," Hyun Jung explained. "Geum San is the county seat, but my home is in Jin San. I don't really know where they are, sir. I just hope they are still alive, somehow."

The Major shook his head and asked, "How did you say you got separated from your family?"

"Well, sir," she said, "I go to school in the West Gate section of Seoul and live on the campus, in the dorm."

"What school?"

"Ewha Girls' Middle School, sir."

"Did you say Ewha Girls' Middle School?"

"Yes, sir," Hyun Jung said, searching the Major's eyes.

"Oh, the dormitory got bombed," the Major said, looking directly into the girl's eyes.

"*Nae?*" Hyun Jung gasped and then, with her both hands covering her whole face, cried, "No!"

"It was this morning," Major Choi continued. "I heard it on the radio, around noon, today."

"No!" Hyun Jung covered her face with both hands and then cried. She was numb to hear about her school dorm being bombed. She immediately thought about her best friend, Eun Ja, and the Kitchen Halmuhni and Grandpa. She knew Eun Ja didn't have any other place to go.

I just hope she is still alive, Hyun Jung thought. As far as the Kitchen Halmuhni and Grandpa were concerned, they had been kind to all the girls at the dorm and worked so hard to feed the girls, even after the Communist soldiers took all the rice away, that day.

Hyun Jung remembered the wrinkled, broad face of the old Kitchen Halmuhni saying goodbye to her as her group walked away from the two-story redbrick dorm building that morning. This was just ten days before. She still remembered vividly what the Kitchen Halmuhni had said when the five girls were leaving: "Be safe, hear?" She then said, "Until we meet again, hear?" Then the Kitchen Halmuhni had followed the girls out of the dorm building to wave goodbye on that quiet, balmy July morning when the five Ewha girls began their journey south to meet up with the South Korean government.

Major Choi noted Hyun Jung's sad face. "You left someone there?"

Hyun Jung didn't say anything. She kept on crying, softly, with both hands covering her face.

Major Choi said, "War is a terrible thing. We must win this one. Then, only then, all will be okay." Hyun Jung nodded her head and slowly stopped crying. "I respect your father a lot. He is in the opposition camp from the president. Your father is a true leader." Hyun Jung thanked the Major, with silence. "Glad you are going home with me tonight and stay with my family in Pohang until I find your father for you."

Hyun Jung felt hopeful for the first time since the Communists took Seoul. This man, the most powerful man in the Eastern Region of the South Korean Army, wanted to help her find her father. *How fortunate,* she thought.

She knew everything would work out for her, just like the Major has been saying. Times like this, Hyun Jung couldn't help but remember what her mother frequently told her ever since she was a little girl, that she was born with a thousand lucks.

"I will begin searching for your father, right away, tomorrow. I think he is in Daegu, now, I am sure." Hyun Jung listened without saying anything. "Yes, the government has been running towards the south ever since it lost Seoul; first, Daejun, then Daegu. There is no other place to retreat to; next, Busan?"

Hyun Jung's heart filled with sadness, like a repeating silent movie … *Eun Ja and the old Kitchen Halmuhni and Grandpa must have been picked up to the sky by the mighty force of the bomb and dropped back down, hard, onto the ground, resulting in their bodies disappearing into the air, like dust.*

25

Driving without Headlights

It was a narrow and meandering country road that hugged the mountain on the left and the Eastern Sea on the right. The night air was cool, and the sky was a dark gray. Without headlights, they continued driving southeast, towards Pohang, in a top-down army jeep, to the home of Major Choi and his family.

Hyun Jung monitored the incessant sound of the cannon blasts coming from the left side, from the mountains up above. And from the ocean, on the right, frogs croaked loudly in the shimmering water. The reflection of the moonlight on the ocean waves helped them to drive without falling into the water.

"Drive carefully," the Major reminded the driver, Kim. He then continued, "We cannot drive fast without the headlights. A lot of people came through the checkpoint today." Major Choi looked at Hyun Jung and said, "You must be tired. Tell me again, when did you all leave Seoul?"

"On July the fifth, sir."

"How about sleeping?" the Major asked. "Where did you all sleep?"

"Well, sir," Hyun Jung began, "we slept when it was too dark to walk, sir."

"You walked until it got dark?"

"Yes, sir. We slept on the roadsides, beside barley fields, on a mountaintop, and in an empty farmhouse, sir."

"Is that right? How about eating?"

"Sir?"

"What did you all do about eating?"

Hyun Jung hesitated a bit and then said, "We didn't think about eating too much, sir."

"Didn't you all get hungry?"

"Well, sir," Hyun Jung began; after a brief pause, she continued, "We were too scared for our lives to think about food, sir. One night, we had chicken and rice at an empty farmhouse we found, but we didn't eat every day, sir."

"You didn't?"

"Most of the time, we were too scared to feel hungry, sir."

"I see," the Major said. He became quiet, as if he had heard too much already. It was sobering, the conditions this little girl must have endured. "You must have lived under the bbahl-gehng-ee," he said.

"Yes, sir, for ten days in Seoul, sir." She added, "And many more days during our walk, sir. Sometimes, we weren't sure which side we were on, sir."

Major Choi understood what she was saying. He turned completely silent and then said, "War is a terrible thing, especially for the children. The Communists are a cruel bunch. They try to take our country and torture our people."

Major Choi reminded the young driver, again, "Drive cautiously."

"Yes, sir."

"Sometimes, these bbahl-gehng-ees hide behind the bushes and jump on you, even while you are driving."

"Yes, sir," the young driver responded.

In a hushed voice, the Major continued, "They are roaming all around us."

Contrary to what was happening up the nearby mountain, the ocean on the right now appeared calm. The reflection of the full moon trembled gently on the ocean water, as if to say, "All's going to be all right."

"We will be home soon. It's a little over an hour now," the Major said, turning his head toward Hyun Jung again. "How old are you, did you say?"

"Thirteen, sir."

"Oh, yes. I am certain that my children will be good to you. You will be the big sister. The oldest, Soon Hee, is just eleven, and her brother, Soon Tae, is nine. You will like their mother, too. She is a good person." The Major then asked, "Any siblings?"

"Yes, sir," Hyun Jung said. "My elder brother, Joong Yul, is in the Korean Army. But I don't know what's happening with him now, sir."

"Is that right?" Major Choi said. "Too bad we cannot have any headlights. The enemy will spot us if we turn the lights on. See, they are all over this mountain."

Hyun Jung listened to everything he said.

"Our government is now in Daegu. I will try to find your father. I will begin looking for him the first thing tomorrow morning. From Seoul, the government first fled to Daejun. It has been in Daegu for the last two weeks or so."

The moon was bright and clear. Its reflection in the ocean was equally clear, like looking into a mirror. The sound of frogs croaking close by was nearly drowned out by the equally incessant sound of the guns and cannons from the nearby mountain. Kim drove the open-top jeep carefully, hugging the mountainside as much as possible on his left, because on the right side, there was no guardrail between the road and the ocean.

"Must try to stay close to the mountain," the Major told the driver.

"Yes, sir," the driver quietly answered.

From the mountains on the left-hand side, the enemies could be eyeing anything that moved. At one point, Major Choi noticed a slight movement from one of those bushes.

"Can you increase the speed a bit?" the Major whispered. He

then turned his head toward Hyun Jung and said, "You must be tired."

"I am okay, sir."

Major Choi was a large man, over six feet tall. But Hyun Jung thought he didn't look too bad. He looked manly in every way. She felt secure with him. She felt as though he would, in fact, find her father for her, as he had been saying since they first met.

The breeze from the ocean softened the fear of attacks from behind the bushes and from the towering mountain on their left. But Hyun Jung knew she must always be alert as to what might happen, any moment, without any forewarning.

26

Pohang Was Still Far Away

Though they were still far away from Pohang, Hyun Jung was glad to see some lights ahead. All the same, they must be getting close to a civilization, with lights. *Maybe we are near where the Major lives,* Hyun Jung thought.

Pohang is a city located at the easternmost shore of South Korea. She had never been there before. Her family was from the South Choong Chung Do, and her childhood experience had been from Jin San to Daejun and to Seoul. Jin San was where she was born and had attended elementary school for about two years, before she was sent away to Daejun at third grade to attend another school, before going up to Seoul to Ewha Girls' Middle School.

The Pohang area was totally new territory for the thirteen-year-old Yu Hyun Jung. She has never been there before and couldn't understand the dialects the people spoke there. In fact, she never had contact with the people from the region. *Well, it's still Korea*, she thought, sitting in the back seat.

After driving for what seemed a never-ending venture in the top-down army jeep, they finally arrived at the Major's house, in Pohang. It was still dark when they arrived, with a few dim lights here and there. Hyun Jung wasn't sure about the place.

The grounds appeared rather large, with several buildings dotted throughout. After parking the jeep, they walked through a small but ornate wooden gate. It was obvious from a glimpse at the layout of the place, it had been some sort of Japanese compound.

The Japanese had occupied Korea from 1910 until 1945, when World War II ended. Hyun Jung still remembered clearly how the Japanese buildings and shrines had looked. To her, they were cold; she never could warm up to the Japanese architecture. She remembered many unpleasant things about them, even though she had been just a young kid then.

The entranceway to the house had a bare minimum of lights. The first thing Hyun Jung noticed as she stepped into the gate was a rock garden with a fish pond. With the help of light reflecting from the Major's family members holding up the lanterns, she saw a large fish swimming and making ripples between the rocks in the rather dark water with irregular light reflections. Stepping onto large rocks, she came closer to the inner part of the house, where several people stood with lanterns to greet them.

Mrs. Choi led her own children and other people who resided at the residential compound to greet the three arrivals. "You all must be hungry," Mrs. Choi cried out. "Walk carefully, just step on the rocks, then you will be fine."

Everyone gathered on the wooden floor at a sliding door that led into the inner part of the house. It was too dark for Hyun Jung to see very well, but she could tell, with the help of the lights from the lanterns, that the front yard was a rock garden with goldfish pond.

"There was no place to eat," Major Choi said to his wife, who was standing next to him holding a lantern. He sat down at the entranceway to take off his shoes before stepping onto the shiny wooden floor that led into yet another part of the house. Hyun Jung followed the Major and took off her shoes and went inside with a young girl, who was smiling from ear to ear.

"Student Aunt, I am going to help you from now on," the girl said and led Hyun Jung to a small bedroom.

Hyun Jung thought Mrs. Choi was very attractive. She was

petite, even for Korean standards, and had short, curly black hair that complemented her almond-shaped face. She moved around the house in a gentle and graceful manner without making any sound.

After hanging up her husband's jacket in the wardrobe closet, Mrs. Choi tiptoed into the kitchen to the Kitchen *Azumma* (aunt), to make sure dinner was ready. The table had already been set with hot soup, steamed rice, and an assortment of banchan (side dishes), ready to be served, just as soon as everyone sat down after freshening up. The three ate their late meal fast, having had no food all day.

At one point, Hyun Jung was mindful of the fact that there were many soldiers at the compound. She made up her mind that she wasn't going to be socializing with any of them. She remembered how her mother used to warn her about guys, saying a girl must carry herself properly. She knew she wasn't going to let any of the young soldiers get the wrong idea about her, like that skinny guy at the checkpoint that night.

"This is your room," Yung Ja, the errand girl, said.

It was a small, empty room with a shiny golden-color floor and no furniture whatsoever, a typical Korean bedroom.

Yung Ja finger-brushed her short black pageboy-style hair and then said, "See this large window? That's the north side of the room. It's a big window, from wall to wall."

Hyun Jung guessed that Yung Ja was also about thirteen years old, like herself.

She noticed the colorful silk bedding and a pillow when Yung Ja slid open the closet door. "You must be tired," Yung Ja said sympathetically. "In the morning, when you get up, come to the dining hall for breakfast. Remember where we had dinner tonight?"

Hyun Jung nodded.

Yung Ja continued, "Sleep well, Student Azumma," and disappeared after sliding the door closed behind her.

Hyun Jung was glad she was alone, finally. Moreover, she

was thankful she didn't have to sleep in a barley field on top of a mountain, behind roadside bushes, or in an abandoned farmhouse.

Even though she was grateful she was there, inside of a house, Hyun Jung wasn't really sure how safe the place was. Still, she was tired from the long drive and those ten days of walking, and she was glad she could lie down in a room with four walls and a ceiling to protect her from straying bullets.

27

Home and Jail

On the first day at Major Choi's house in Pohang, Hyun Jung was awakened by Yung Ja's hollering, "Student *azumma*, Auntie. Please get up; breakfast is served."

"Who?" Hyun Jung didn't respond immediately, but after a few minutes, she realized Yung Ja was calling her to breakfast.

Hyun Jung rolled the mat she had slept on and folded the comforter she used the night before. To make it complete, she placed the pillow on the top of the mat and comforter, and then placed them all in the closet behind a set of sliding doors, as Yung Ja had told her to do just last night. At first, Hyun Jung wasn't sure who the student *azumma* was. She had been called kkoma (kid) by her group for all those ten intensive days of walking. Finally, she realized that Student azumma was herself.

"Hurry, come. Your breakfast is getting cold. Come to the dining hall, please."

Needless to say, it took Hyun Jung some adjusting to do from being called kkoma, kid, to Student azumma, auntie.

The city of Pohang was located on the Eastern Sea in North Kyung Sang Do. This city was also called Busan Perimeter. The city grew around the spacious KCIA headquarters. Major Choi, his wife, and their two children, along with layers of military and civilian personnel, lived together on this large housing compound. Everyone slept, ate, and worked there in this war-ravaged country.

Having lost important Major cities up north like Seoul and Daejun to the Communist invaders, Pohang played an important role in what was left of the Republic of Korea, also known as South Korea.

The front part of the compound served as the headquarters of the Korean CIA for the Eastern Region. Major Choi was the top boss for the whole region.

The north side of the compound had one long row of a building that seemed haphazardly put together. It was constructed of unpainted, rough wooden boards, rusted metal sheets, unmatched building posts, and the sort, definitely, a makeshift wartime structure.

As Hyun Jung tiptoed into the dining hall, she noticed how clean the wooden floor was. It was in various shades of gold. What a change from just one day before, when she and her group from Seoul walked down the dusty, refugee-packed highway.

The Kitchen Azumma prepared a healthy-looking breakfast with an assortment of *banchan*. The breakfast included grilled fish carefully garnished with thinly sliced red pepper, lettuce, and chrysanthemum leaves. The table reminded Hyun Jung of meals at her own home in Jin San when she was growing up.

A roomful of uniformed young soldiers was seated around the rectangular table on the floor. They had already started eating when Hyun Jung arrived. All of them, without exception, acknowledged her arrival with polite nods. Seeing these soldiers didn't take Hyun Jung aback. After all, she had been seeing uniformed soldiers from both the North and the South Korean sides here and there since that day when the Communists invaded Seoul.

Hyun Jung quietly looked for Mr. and Mrs. Choi but didn't see either one of them, anywhere. She thought, *They must have a separate breakfast table in a separate room.* She joined the others at the large table, sitting at the prearranged spot for her. A customary set of bronze spoon and chopsticks waited for her at the spot. Hyun Jung noticed the Kitchen Azumma glancing at her rather frequently.

"Begin with your soup," the Kitchen Azumma said, placing a bowl in front of the young girl. "Did you sleep well, Student Azumma?"

Hyun Jung answered politely with a nod and soft *"nae"* (Yes, ma'am). The Kitchen Azumma continued, "Poor thing, not even knowing where her parents are." Before Hyun Jung could answer, the Kitchen Azumma said, "You must be tired. It's not your fault, all that walking for ten days, from Seoul. Aigoo!" The Kitchen Azumma shook her head, which was covered with curly black hair under a black hairnet, and looked at Hyun Jung with sad eyes. "Aigoo, poor thing. Go ahead, eat a lot, slowly. Eat a lot."

Hyun Jung quietly sucked in her answer, "Yes, ma'am." During the whole time she was eating, she didn't say a word to anyone at the table. She ate all her food quietly and got up after putting her spoon and the chopsticks back down on the table.

She didn't even like eating with her dorm mates when she was at Ewha; she liked even less having to share her meal table with a bunch of strange men, soldiers or no soldiers. She missed her life in Jin San, where she shared meals only with her grandfather or her mother.

After breakfast, Hyun Jung went straight back to her room. In the room, she placed herself on the south side of the room, facing north. She had a wide view of the outside through the large glass window. From there, she stared straight out. At first, she didn't see anything. The whole place was silent. There was no sign of any kind. In fact, for many days, the sound of the artillery from the nearby mountains had been her constant companion during her awakened hours.

28

Seeing a Western Man for the First Time

The next morning, following his breakfast, Major Choi left for Daegu. The sole purpose of the trip was to search for Hyun Jung's father, Chairman Yu Chin San. Daegu was about fifty miles southwest from his home in Pohang. Major Choi was certain Yu Chin San was in Daegu. He also was certain that the government of the Republic of Korea had settled itself in Daegu after being pushed out of Seoul. The South Korean government wasn't able to stay in Daejun very long. They had to run away farther south from the surging North Korean Communist army.

Even on the second day at Major Choi's house, Hyun Jung didn't see the Major. She wondered where he was, but she felt sort of out of place to ask about the head of the household. Therefore, she simply kept quiet and just wondered.

The next day, Hyun Jung was a bit more relaxed. After breakfast, she returned to her room. She was not as frightened as she had been since the invasion. Even though she didn't know what was going on with the Major and whether he would find her father, she felt safer than she had felt in a long time. In fact, she welcomed the quiet, uneventful mornings. Hyun Jung idly looked out the large window on the north side of the room, directly in front of her. At first, she didn't see anything special. Unlike what was going on in the country, it was peaceful and quiet. Just another bright July morning, that was not considered to be out of the ordinary, she thought.

That tranquility, however, wasn't to last very long. Around nine o'clock, she saw something she had never seen before. She looked out the window, and about fifty feet away, she saw two men, both wearing dark color clothing, struggling with each other. Hyun Jung held her breath and inched over closer to the window. Then, she saw something that took all her attention. One man had a stick in his hand and was dragging the other man by the collar. Hyun Jung moved closer to the scene.

The man doing the dragging shouted, "You are a bbahl-gehng-ee!?"

"No, sir."

"What do you mean, no?" the man with a stick shouted and continued, "You are a Commie. Isn't that true?"

"Aigoo. ... No, sir," the other man cried. He kept his head down and his both hands raised above his head to protect his skull. He then cried with both hands covering his whole face.

"You bastard, tell the truth. You are a bbahl-gehng-ee, aren't you?"

"No ... sir," the man wailed loudly, again. "Aigoo. ... No, sir."

The man with the stick pulled the other man by his collar and beat him here and there, like dusting an old blanket.

"Aigoo. Aigoo," the man cried, covering his face with his arms. "No, sir."

Hyun Jung bowed her head. She was troubled to watch a man getting beat up with a stick, as if he didn't have any feelings. However, after wrestling it over, she rationalized these happenings were a part of the war between the Communists invaders and the democratic South Koreans. *War brings about many problems for people,* she thought. *But the invaders are the wrong party, and the Republic of Korea was right for being watchful of the Communist troublemakers.* Still, the scene was quite troubling to the thirteen-year-old Yu Hyun Jung.

The next day at the Major's house was the same: After her breakfast, Hyun Jung returned to her empty room. She took a seat at exactly the same spot, on the south side of the room, as she had done the day before, and looked out through the large glass window directly on the north side of the room. Again, the noise began. As she had done the day before, she quietly inched closer to the window on the north side of the room, to hear if anything was different from yesterday.

She saw two men again. One held a thick stick in his hand. He was dressed in a dark-blue uniform with matching dark color cap. The man with the stick went into one of the cells.

Next, Hyun Jung noticed the same tall, skinny man being dragged out by the man with the thick stick. The man was being held by his shirt collar, like the day before. Once the two men came out of the cell, the man with the stick started to beat the other man's back, shoulder, and every place he could reach. The man was crying and tried to protect his head with his two hands and arms, pleading for mercy. However, the man with the stick continued his beating, demanding, in a loud voice, "You bastard, tell the truth. You are a bbahl-gehng-ee, aren't you?"

"Aigoo, aigoo," the man wailed. "No, sir."

The man with the stick continued with his beating. "You are a bbahl-gehng-ee. Why do you lie to me? Don't think you can fool me. I know what you are."

"No, sir," the man cried, with both of his hands covering his tilted head.

"You better admit it, understand?" the man with the stick shouted. "If not, I'll have to use this stick until it splits your thick skull into pieces."

"No, sir, I am not a bbahl-gehng-ee, sir."

"What do you mean, no?" The man with the stick continued to beat on the accused. "Are you fooling me? Do you think this is some kind of kid's game?"

After watching the two men for a while, Hyun Jung returned to her original spot, on the south side of the room. She was troubled to see a human being getting beat up, as if he didn't have any feelings. Hyun Jung became sad and started thinking philosophically.

After a while, however, Hyun Jung felt more rested and was glad she had the protection, security, and comfort of the Major's walls.

Around ten in the morning, Hyun Jung heard, "Come, Unnee [Big Sister], come out and play with us."

"Yeah, please," Hyun Jung heard Soon Tae's voice.

It was Soon Hee. Hyun Jung went out and joined Soon Hee and Soon Tae. These kids treated Hyun Jung well. They called her Unnee, Big Sister, because she was the oldest among the three.

Hyun Jung welcomed the change.

The kids weren't allowed to leave the wall of their home ground, but they could play freely as long as they stayed within the locked gate of the stone wall. The two Choi family children obeyed their parents and stayed inside of this large, enclosed compound that was built with stone and tile. The gates were kept locked, night and day.

The parents were protective of their two young children. During wartime, they especially didn't want their children to see what went on in the outside world. They didn't want the children exposed to the street scenes. They really didn't want them to be exposed to loose women, holding hands and chewing gum and walking with Westerners like Yankee soldiers, in broad daylight. Even for the wartime, this was an unsightly scene for the tradition-bound Korean people. Since the war broke out in June, some strange things were going on all over the city. The parents knew there was a nightclub across the street. In the minds of the parents, the nightclub was where the soldiers drank liquor and had sex with loose women. Evil activities were happening in this nightclub. The parents were sure of that.

The children of the Choi family were not allowed to know such places existed. They were simply to be confined within the walls.

"Stay inside the wall," their mother reminded them, when she went out for an errand. "You are not supposed to go outside of this wall. You both understand, don't you?" These were her routine reminders to the children whenever she and Yung Ja stepped out to do food shopping.

When they climbed up to the second-floor rock garden, Soon Hee and Soon Tae ran directly to the front part of the tatami mat room. They took spots by the small rice paper sliding doors that opened up directly to the city's main street. Soon Hee and Hyun Jung quietly opened the small sliding window that opened onto the busy city. "Shee!" Soon Hee said, her hands covering her mouth.

Then, Soon Hee quickly slammed the door shut when she saw a large Western soldier walking with a stocky, curly-haired Korean woman. They were walking together on the street, in broad daylight.

This was the very first time Hyun Jung saw a Western man. Sure, she had seen Western women, like the two English conversation teachers at her school, Miss Martin and Mrs. Sour, but they were women. She didn't know what to think of the soldier with white skin and yellow hair. Both the man and the woman were chewing something and walking, hand in hand, toward the nightclub. Hyun Jung was scared and whispered, forcefully, "Let's go."

The three children ran out of the room just as fast as if a hungry bear was chasing them.

29

Han River Bridge

After being on the front line all morning, Yu Chin San returned to Kookje Hotel in downtown Daegu. The hotel had been his home away from home for the last two weeks or so. He lived there alone, like many other men who fled Seoul to avoid being captured by the Communist invaders.

Since he took off from Seoul that unforgettable day, his thoughts were sad. He deeply regretted that before running away from the city, he hadn't gone to the West Gate section of Seoul to collect Hyun Jung. She was his only daughter, and he loved her very much. A day didn't go by when he didn't think about her. She was just thirteen years old, a kid.

He remembered the day very vividly. That morning, he had walked into the office building where his friend, Dr. Min Byung Soo, the Minister of Home Affairs, is located on the third floor. When he got out of the third-floor elevator, Dr. Min had, without a word, pulled Yu across the hallway into his office and then whispered, "We must cross the Han River Bridge, now, as soon as possible."

"Yes?"

"Before it gets bombed."

Yu Chin San had looked straight at the Minister's eyes without a word. Dr. Min had continued, "Hurry up, if you don't want to get caught and executed by bbahl-gehng-ee."

As one of the cabinet members in Rhee Seung Mahn's administration, Dr. Min had known the government's plan to bomb the bridge over the Han River. This would stop the Communists from crossing the river and marching down toward the southern part of the country.

"Oh?" Yu Chin San had said. "But I must go and get my daughter from her school."

"Where's the school?"

"The West Gate section."

"We can come back for her later. We must take off, right now. The enemies are almost in Seoul already. They crossed the DMZ [Demilitarized Zone], 38th Parallel, last night."

Dr. Min's hushed voice was forceful and urgent. Yu Chin San knew immediately what he was saying.

Yu also knew too well how close the DMZ was: only thirty-five miles north of Seoul.

Many families in the capital city were separated during this wartime. Typically, the elderly and the very young were left behind with womenfolk, but the young sons were at the battlefields, and the men went into hiding or fled for their lives.

Since the war broke out, like most men in South Korea, Yu Chin San was estranged from his family. His elderly father was still in his province home, Jin San, and his wife was also there, as far as he knew.

He had not heard from them since the war broke out. His wife had gone down to Jin San to take care of matters after the big Parliamentary election in May, where he was defeated by the woman candidate, Tae Jung Shin.

His thirteen-year-old daughter remained at the dorm in her school, in Seoul. He hadn't heard anything about Joong Yul, his son, who was in South Korean Army fighting the Communist guerillas at the southern tip of Ji Ri Mountain. But on June 25, since the war broke out, he knew this situation was not unusual. In fact, it was rather typical of many men in the country after that day, when the Communist North sneakily and, yet, swiftly invaded the South.

With heavy heart, Yu Chin San closed his eyes when he learned the Ewha Girls' Middle School dormitory had been bombed. He felt helpless and tried not to be too remorseful about his situation. He knew too well he was sharing this same wartime tragedy with the majority of the men in the country.

Actually, he had no idea of the whereabouts of his wife, either. And a little boy, Han Yul, who had been with his mother in Jin San. He worried about his elderly father, still in Jin San, his mountainous hometown. Jin San was located near Ji Ri Mountain, where the Communist guerillas frequently raided and raised havoc in the small farming village. He endured the situation by trying not to think about it. Whenever he thought about the situation of the country, he appreciated the young soldiers who were at the front line, fighting the enemies.

But more than once, Yu Chin San had closed his eyes to cry quietly for his daughter. That little girl he loved so much must now be dead from the bombing, which he heard about through the radio. Hyun Jung was not in this world anymore. He was certain of that. He had been living with a heavy heart since that fateful day he crossed the Han River Bridge with Dr. Min, without his daughter, Hyun Jung.

Now, the dorm has been bombed, he thought. He frequently let out a big sigh whenever he thought about her. She was one child he was very happy with. He had sons, but she was his favorite. His own elderly father had often said, "That girl will amount to something, someday."

His hometown, Jin San, was now completely in the hands of the Communists. Yu Chin San was certain of that. The town was so close to Ji Ri Mountain, where the Communist guerilla agitation had been fierce even before the invasion, on June 25, 1950.

Like many refugees who fled without family members, Yu Chin

San often found himself wondering what was happening with his elderly father, his wife, and his children. His eldest son was now serving the country by fighting the Communists in the battle zone at the Ji Ri Mountain. He could only hope and pray that all of them were alive, somehow, somewhere.

Yu Chin San was certain that the Communists would have executed him if he hadn't fled Seoul, as his friend, Dr. Min, had urged him to do.

All the same, he felt guilty for not being with his family in this time of distress.

30

Search

For nine days, since he brought Hyun Jung to his house, Major Choi had searched Daegu, the new seat of the fleeing South Korean government. The streets were packed with refugees. No one could help the Major find the man he was trying to find. The sea of people, mostly men, were milling around aimlessly all over the city.

To start with, he had gone to the office of the Ministry of Home Affairs. Dr. Min was the top man there. Major Choi had read in various newspapers that Yu Chin San and Dr. Min worked closely together. After much trial and error, he glanced at the address of the gray building and went in and came to a small office of the Ministry of Home Affairs. At a small office, Major Choi told the receptionist at the front desk that he was looking for "someone very important."

"Yes?" the receptionist said, looking up right into the Major's eyes from her desk.

"Chairman Yu," Major Choi began. "He is the Chairman of the Anti-Communist League for Korean Youth."

The receptionist thought about it for a while and then said, "You mean, Chairman Yu Chin San?"

"Yes," said the Major, widening his eyes and leaning closer to the young woman at the desk.

"Try Kookje Hotel," the receptionist continued. "All the important government people stay there."

"Kookje Hotel?"

"It's rather far from here. A taxi will take you there, it's too far to walk because of all these people milling around the street." The receptionist then said, "I take it back. In fact, one can walk there faster than a taxi ride; because of the many people, a car would have a harder time ploughing through."

"It's okay," Major Choi said. He was insistent on getting to the hotel as soon as he could.

The young receptionist went back to working on her typewriter, took a brief pause, and said, "Just keep going on the road right front of this building, turn left, and you will come to a crossroad. Take the right, then keep going until you come to the hotel."

Major Choi grew confident that now, finally, he would be able to locate Hyun Jung's father, as he had promised the young girl. He felt that he made a significant progress and decided to call his wife in Pohang to let her know what he had accomplished.

"Not yet," he said to his wife over the phone. "You should see this place. People are all over. No one seems to know what to do. They are just milling around."

"Aigoo," his wife sympathized. "You are having such a hard time. I hope you don't forget to eat your meals on time. Don't forget your lunch."

"I won't. I'll keep on looking. Don't tell Hyun Jung. Don't say anything to her, yet. She needs some hope, poor girl." Then he added, "She lost both her parents."

After the phone call to his wife, Major Choi joined the sea of people on the streets of Daegu and tried to follow what the young receptionist had told him. He was determined to locate Yu Chin San, but he decided to get a quick bite of lunch, first. He went back to his jeep and told his driver, Kim, to go and get some lunch, too.

Inside a small windowless noodle shop, Sam Sung Gook Soo (Three Star Noodle House), Major Choi noticed a young man with his face buried behind a newspaper. He thought, *He must pay attention to what's going on in the government.*

After ordering *naeng myun* (cold buckwheat noodle), the Major took a quick survey of the place. Then, he walked over to the young man at the table with the newspaper and said, "Excuse me, young man."

The young man put the paper down on the table and looked up to the Major, then responded, "Yes?"

"Young man," Major Choi said, standing close, "by any chance, do you know Chairman Yu Chin San?"

Without hesitation, the young man said, "Oh, yes." The young man then said, still holding the newspaper with one hand, "I know about Chairman Yu, but …"

"I need to locate him."

"You need to locate him?"

"Yes; do you know who I am talking about?"

"Oh, yes," the young man said, putting the newspaper down on the table. "I know from reading the newspapers that he is a good friend of Dr. Min Byung Soo, the Minister of Home Affairs."

"Is that right? I need to find Chairman Yu," Major Choi said impatiently to the young man.

A waiter, an old man with a slim face and a missing front tooth, brought a small tray of food to the young man's table. He then carefully placed the small dishes of banchan on the table.

"*Ajuhssi* [Uncle]," the young man with the newspaper said to the old waiter, "This officer," he glanced at the Major's freshly pressed uniform and army insignia, "is looking for Chairman Yu Chin San. Do you know how to find him, by any chance?"

"Yes, I know," the old man said immediately, as if he was waiting for the question. "He comes here sometimes. I believe he is staying at the Kookje Hotel. It's not too far from here." The waiter pointed with his narrow chin toward the direction of the hotel.

"Oh?" the Major said. "Is that the biggest hotel in town?"

Balancing the tray on one hand, the old man said, "Yes, many important people are staying there. I will take you there. With so many people on the street, it's hard to find anything or any place, anymore." The old man waiter then said, "Let me take off this apron." He then rushed back to the kitchen and untied his apron.

"I will compensate you for your time," the Major said. This made the old waiter very happy. After paying for his lunch, he rushed out the door, walking right next to the old man. Together, they searched for the Kookje Hotel.

The two men began walking in the crowded Daegu street. They both were satisfied that they were making progress in this crowded street. But soon, Major Choi looked for the old man, but he was nowhere to be seen. When the Major turned back, there he was, having a squabble with a young man who was angry at the toothless old waiter.

"I already told you it was an accident," the young man said to the old waiter. "I didn't mean to brush against your side."

Major Choi was glad it didn't take too long for the old man to come back. "What's the matter, Grandfather?"

"Just that, that young guy accused me of poking him with my elbow."

"Just too many people for this city, I guess," Major Choi said.

The old man shook his head and calmed himself down, and said, "Do you see that black iron gate on the hill? That's part of the hotel ... Kookje Hotel."

Most of the refugees on the street were men. If women made it to this city, they would stay back at their shelter and let the menfolk go out and see what was going on in this packed city. There wasn't even an inch of room to move around without bumping into or brushing against somebody.

Major Choi finally noticed a small sign for Kookje Hotel in *Hangul* (Korean script). The Major was relieved and said to the old waiter, "Here you are. I have been looking for Yu Chin San for the last two whole days, and you find the place where he stays in less than one hour."

The old waiter was happy because he knew he had done his good deed for the day by helping the Major find Yu Chin San.

After getting a generous payment from the Major, the old waiter light-heartedly walked back to his job at the Three Star Noodle Shop.

"You just missed him," the man at the hotel said and introduced the Major to another man. "Here is Mr. Jung, Chairman Yu Chin San's secretary."

"Oh, so sorry," the secretary said. "Chairman Yu took off with the Minister, Dr. Min Byung Soo, for the daily frontline inspection."

"Oh, I finally found him," Major Choi said. "I finally located him."

"What are you talking about?" Mr. Jung asked.

"I have his daughter; you see?"

"What?"

"She was roaming around at the frontline, a war zone, a checkpoint," the Major said, searching the secretary's eyes.

"*Aigoo!*" The secretary frowned his dark eyes, then shook his head.

"Lost!"

"Aigoo!"

"I brought her to my house."

"You did?" Mr. Jung said, with his eyes stretched wide. "Chairman Yu will be very grateful. You did a good deed."

"I will just wait for the Chairman to return," Major Choi said. "Now I know I found him."

With glee, Major Choi called his wife at home in Pohang. "I found him," he exclaimed. "I found Hyun Jung's father."

"Have you seen him?"

"No, not yet. He went out with Minister Dr. Min Byung Soo to inspect the frontline."

"I knew you'd find him," his wife said. "I had all the confidence you would locate the Chairman."

"Nobody knows when he will be back, though," Major Choi said into the phone, lowering his voice.

"Don't go anywhere," his wife said. "Wait there until the Chairman returns."

31

Checkpoint?

As Chairman Yu Chin San entered his hotel lobby, Secretary Jung stepped closer and whispered, "There is a visitor waiting for you, sir."

"Uh?" Yu was alarmed. "Who?"

"An army officer, sir. He has been waiting for you for a long while, sir. He says it's very important, sir."

"Who is it?"

"He is the KCIA director, sir. The top man of Pohang Division, sir."

"Show him in," Yu Chin San told Mr. Jung.

While the Chairman stepped out to freshen up, the secretary brought Major Choi into the large tatami mat room.

When he returned to his room, Yu Chin San nodded to the Major and pointed to one of the deep-blue silk cushions placed in front of the guest.

"Have a seat, have a seat, please," Yu Chin San said.

Major Choi took one of the silk cushions and sat down.

Yu asked, "How can I help you?"

"Sir ... well ... sir," Major Choi said, hesitating a bit. Then, he continued, "It's about your daughter, sir."

"What?" Yu Chin San widened his dark eyes, stiffened a bit, and asked, "What about my daughter?"

"Miss Hyun Jung, sir ..."

"How!? … Did you?" Instantly, his forehead wrinkled and with stretched dark eyes, he stuttered, "Yah … a … h!"

"We found her at a battlefield checkpoint, sir."

"Checkpoint? What checkpoint? Where?" Yu Chin San asked, staring at the guest. "I thought when her school got bombed, she was …"

"She walked for ten days, all the way from Seoul, sir."

"What?"

"Yes, sir."

"Oh, my," Yu Chin San said, wiping tears with a white handkerchief. "Where is she now?"

"She is at my house, sir."

"Your house?" Yu covered his face and wiped more tears.

"I am sorry, sir," the Major said and waited for Yu to collect himself.

No one spoke. Finally, Yu began, "The day the Communists took Seoul, I couldn't go over to her school on the West Gate section of the city and get her."

"I understand, sir," the Major said. "The enemy took Seoul so swiftly, sir."

Yu continued, "Where did you meet my daughter?"

"At that frontline checkpoint, for Pohang Division, sir."

"How did she get there?" Yu Chin San was curious about everything, how his daughter ended up with this man sitting front of him.

"She had been walking with some other students, sir."

"Oh." Yu Chin San was a bit calmer now. "Where is your house?"

"Pohang, sir."

"Let's go," Yu Chin San said, getting up from his cushion. "I need to see my daughter." He placed both hands on his face and said, "But we must first make a tour to the battle zone. So many young men are making sacrifices to protect this country from the invaders."

He had visited the battle zone earlier today but didn't feel right putting his own personal happiness first, when the young men were making such sacrifices to protect the country.

"Ninety-nine percent of Korean men are without family. How can I care only about my own happiness?"

"Yes, sir," the Major said, lowering his head.

"I would like to see my daughter, but I'm not the only one with family scattered all over this country, not knowing when they will see each other again," Yu Chin San said, buttoning his khaki shirt. "At least my daughter came to me, and that makes me luckier than anyone I know."

"I owe you a debt of gratitude," the Chairman said, looking at the Major.

"Not at all, sir," the Major said. "Your daughter is such a remarkable young lady, sir. Walking for ten days, all the way from Seoul."

Yu Chin San went to the back of the room to get ready to return to the battle zone. In the meantime, Major Choi contacted Captain Woo at the front line near Pohang and told him he was bringing Yu Chin San. "Have a simple supper for about five people," the Major told Captain Woo. Then he looked at his watch and placed a quick call to his wife. "I finally located Hyun Jung's father," he said.

"I knew you'd be able to do just that," she said. "You did well, Soon Hee's father."

"Can you have dinner ready for everyone?"

"Of course!"

"Chairman Yu and his entourage, a secretary and a driver, and my two men, about six people altogether."

"Don't worry, everything will be perfect," Mrs. Choi said. "Just don't worry about things like that!"

"Do you know what this means to our family?" Major Choi asked his wife of sixteen happy years.

"I know," Mrs. Choi said. "This would open doors for us to the upper crust of Korean society. Ordinarily, we wouldn't have such an opportunity. You were lucky you met Hyun Jung that day at the checkpoint." She continued, "Just don't worry about the dinner, Soon Hee's father. The dinner will be ready when you arrive, whatever time that might be."

The Major told his wife, "First, we'll go to the front line to see how the young soldiers are doing. Afterward, we'll head home. It might be around midnight."

"Everything will be ready."

"The enemy fights at night," he explained. "I want to show Chairman Yu the soldiers in action. The enemy is sneaky. They only come out at night."

"I understand," his wife continued. "Everything will be ready when you arrive. Just be careful."

Major Choi thought about how fortunate he was to have married such an understanding, able, and willing wife.

"He is such a great man," the Major continued. "He appreciates our fighting young men and said he couldn't put his personal life ahead of the young soldiers who are fighting for this country."

"Of course, he is right, Soon Hee's father," his wife said. "Be careful, always. We'll be ready to receive the guests."

As the wife of a high-ranking army officer, who happened to be the top man in the Battle of Busan Perimeter of the Republic of Korea, Mrs. Choi was skilled at keeping up with her husband's military, social, and personal life. She had numerous live-in helpers and soldiers who worked for her husband. She had to feed and manage the welfare of every single one of them who were now away from home and family. She carried out some twenty-plus individuals sharing the compound with grace and pleasantness, while raising two young children of her own. The Major knew he was one of the luckiest men alive; unlike most of the men he knew, he was able to keep his family with him, even during wartime.

32

The News

Hyun Jung was walking through the inner part of the compound, along with Soon Hee and Soon Tae, when she heard Mrs. Choi calling, "Hyun Jung?"

"N*eh*?" Hyun Jung responded, pausing from her walk.

"Major Choi found your father."

"*Neh*?"

"Yes; you will see him later this evening when he gets home." Hyun Jung listened without any interruption. "First, he has to inspect the battlefields, then the Major will bring him home."

"Yes, ma'am."

"He will be here with his own driver and a secretary."

Hyun Jung was very excited. In fact, she was too excited and prayed that nothing would happen, like having to run away from the Communists before she had the chance to see her father again. It was almost too good to be true. She could hear her mother's quiet loving voice, saying, "My daughter was born with a thousand lucks," as she did whenever good things came her way. She recalled hearing her mother tell this to one of their neighbors who was visiting. She heard this many times from a very young age. Whenever she found herself in danger, she would think about her mother's loving eyes looking at her. Hyun Jung treasured her mother's sayings like, "No greater luck," about her only daughter. She knew she had such a loving mother.

She had lived under the Communists in Seoul until they took all the rice away from her dorm, and then she walked for ten days in a refugee-covered highway, hearing the gunshots from nearby battlefields. She still was proud to learn her father was alive and safe, but even more, that he continued with his important work for the country. *Of course, he had to make the tour of the frontline first, however much he wanted to see his long-lost daughter. The young soldiers were fighting for the country.* She knew that much about her father. To him, the country came even before his family.

Major Choi called Captain Woo again. "We'll be there this evening. Will everything be ready? I am bringing with me Chairman Yu Chin San of the Anti-Communist League, you know."

"Yes, sir," Captain Woo said. "The enemy is just over the mountain, sir. I can hear their gunshots, but we are holding them back, sir."

"Good, keep it up," Major Choi told Lieutenant Woo.

"Good that you will be here in the evening, sir," Captain Woo said. "There is no action during the daytime, but they get active in the night, sir."

Standing nearby Major Choi, Yu Chin San overheard what the Captain said and remarked, "That's right. I knew that. The Communists are like bedbugs. They only come out at night, in the dark."

It was around six o'clock in the evening; the summer sun was still lingering in the western sky when the Major and the Chairman arrived at the battlefield. Yu Chin San and Major Choi put their helmets on before walking out to the battleground. After a brief greeting by bowing to each other, Captain Woo led the guests onto the battleground for a brief inspection. Afterwards, they shared a quick meal consisting of steamed rice, beef broth soup, and kimchi at the cafeteria tent in the army barracks. A few other uniformed soldiers were served at the same table as well.

"We already knew, sir." The Captain said as soon as he took the chair next to the Major. "The report from Daegu approached this compound early, sir. Everyone respects Chairman Yu for his anti-Communist activities, sir."

Captain Woo bowed to the Chairman.

After dinner, Yu shook hands with the Captain and told him how much he appreciated the sacrifice he was making. He then shook hands with the young soldiers and thanked them too.

At the home of Major Choi, the entire family stayed up and waited for the entourage to arrive. No one in the family went to sleep; that would be showing disrespect for the guests. The whole family, including the kitchen helpers and the three children, Soon Hi, Soon Tae, and Hyun Jung, dutifully waited.

Finally, around eleven that night, Major Choi, Chairman Yu, and their men arrived at the home of Major Choi in Pohang.

After all these turbulent months, when they didn't know whether each other was alive or dead, Hyun Jung greeted her father with a deep bow from a proper distance of about five feet away. In return, as it was the Korean custom, her father acknowledged her with a nod and a quiet but big smile.

"Of course. Of course," her father said.

The truth was, actually, Hyun Jung didn't know him very well. He had been away to China to work for the Korean government in exile there during the Japanese occupation of Korea. The Japanese would put him in jail if they caught him. To the thirteen-year-old girl, he was more like an important guest, but a distant one. He had been absent for too many years when she was a young child. She did not remember seeing him until she was nine years of age, when he returned home after Japan's World War II surrender in 1945. Fear of retribution against them, the defeated Japanese immediately fled Korea like facing a tsunami warning after a strong earthquake.

To the thirteen-year-old Hyun Jung, her father was really a stranger. In her mind, a father was like a very important houseguest. He simply wasn't around enough when she was growing up, even to this day.

Yu Chin San had fought against the Japanese occupation of Korea, and the occupiers were constantly trying to interrogate him and to put him in jail for his anti-Japanese activities. As a young man, though, he was educated at Waseda University in Tokyo, where he majored in English and Economics. He opposed the Japanese occupation and became a civil rights attorney after college. In this capacity, he helped to negotiate release of Korean political prisoners out of the Japanese jails. In addition, his own father also opposed the Japanese occupation and supported the Korean government in exile in Chong Ching, China. Moreover, Yu Chin San (then Yu Yung Pil) wrote a book for Korean farmers, suggesting they set up their own credit unions instead of paying high interest and service charges to the Japanese-owned banks.

Consequently, he himself was imprisoned. In fact, he was put in prison seven different times during the thirty-six years of the Japanese occupation of Korea.

Hyun Jung didn't know all these things about her father. Her family had sent her to a city school to learn to mingle with girls from more sophisticated families. First, she was sent to Dae Heung Elementary School in Daejun at the age of nine. Later, at age twelve, she was sent to Ewha Girls' Middle School in Seoul and lived on campus.

Now, she would have to get used to being a daughter to her long-lost father. In a real sense, she didn't know him very well. More importantly, she wasn't familiar with her role as a daughter.

In the large guest room at Major Choi's home, the lamps were bright enough for the two men to carry on their conversation all night. To celebrate finding Hyun Jung, the two men drank *sojoo*, Korean hard liquor, until they fell asleep.

Many Korean men drank to show their deep sorrow. In this respect, Yu Chin San was no exception. Yu repeated in a slightly slurred tone of voice, "I couldn't go to fetch my only daughter, when the Communists invaded Seoul." The Major sat directly in front of his guest, with his head down to show respect. He continued, "Her school was on the West Gate part of Seoul. Dr. Min Byung Soo, the Minister of Home Affairs, insisted that we must cross the Han River Bridge before it got bombed. But she is my only daughter." His voice began breaking. "Only one, not half, not two, only one. She is very special to me."

"Of course, sir," the Major said, and using two hands, to show respect, he poured more sojoo out of the green bottle for his guest.

"Dr. Min also told me we could go back and fetch my daughter when things calmed down." Yu Chin San's voice broke with emotion. Drinking many bottles of sojoo contributed to his slurred speech. "I felt really troubled."

"Yes, sir," Major Choi responded, quietly lowering his head.

The host lowered his head and then quietly poured yet another glass of sojoo.

When he noticed his guest dozing off, Major Choi tiptoed out of the room and closed the sliding door behind himself.

Early the next morning, at Mrs. Choi's suggestion, Hyun Jung quietly tiptoed into the room where her father had been waiting to see her. He was already sitting up and waiting for her to enter the room.

When she stepped into the room, she could smell the cigarettes. She eyed a pile of cigarette butts in the large brass ashtray and also saw a pile of empty green sojoo bottles.

She kneeled in front of her father and bowed to him.

He began talking: "I apologize for not collecting you at your school, that day."

She listened without saying anything.

"It's that Dr. Min Byung Soo insisted that we take off before the Han River Bridge got bombed, and he said we could come back and collect you later, when things got calmer."

Hyun Jung didn't say a word while he spoke. She was just glad her father hadn't been caught by the Communists. Actually, she was grateful to Dr. Min for saving her father's life from the vicious Communists.

33

Joong Yul in Hospital

Riding in a military jeep on an unpaved, crooked dusty road, driven by the Chairman Yu Chin San's driver, Mr. Sohn, they arrived at the Kookje Hotel in Daegu. It actually took about two hours to drive from Major Choi's home in Pohang, where Yu Chin San was reunited with Hyun Jung; he thought he would never see his daughter again when he left Seoul that day the Communist North invaded the capital city, Seoul.

Hyun Jung was happy and contented just to be with her father. She felt as though she had arrived at a point in life where she should have been all along. Now that she was with her father, she didn't feel any danger, just safe and protected. She knew she didn't have to act mature and try to keep up with her group. Still, it was troubling to see so many frightened Korean people milling aimlessly around the crowded streets of Daegu.

With all the refugees pouring in from the north, Daegu had grown to over two million since the war broke just two months before. The masses of people on the street and every corner of the city reminded Hyun Jung of the refugees on the highway.

Kookje Hotel was located right in the middle of Daegu. The city had grown around the hotel. From the window of the living room, one could watch the street scene. More than anything else, the white-clad Korean men were everywhere. Their desperate, defeated facial expressions reflected the state of the South Korean government. The people were just contented to find a shady spot anywhere they could, like the small trees on the side of the road. The only thing for them to do was to wait out what their fleeing government would do next.

When Yu Chin San stepped into the hallway of the hotel lobby, Secretary Jung approached him and said, "Your son is in the hospital, sir."

"What?" Yu Chin San asked, surprised. "Where?"

"The Army Hospital, sir," Secretary Jung continued. "He was injured by the enemy artillery at the Ji Ri Mountain battle zone, sir."

Yu Chin San turned to his daughter and said, "Let's go, your brother is in the hospital."

Even though Yu Chin San was born into a yangban (aristocratic) family in South Choong Chung Do, his life had been anything but predictable and safe. This fifty-four-year-old scion of Yu Kyung Duck Gong of Moon Wah Yu family and Kim Kyung Won of Kwang San Kim clan had spent the last fifty-plus years riding the wave of Korea's tumultuous history.

From the time he was just five years old, in 1910, the year Japan officially occupied Korea, his father taught him never to forget the sacrifices Korean patriots made for the country. As a small boy, Yu Chin San (original name: Yu Yung Pil) had accompanied his father to a gravesite near his hometown, Jin San. There, his father told the young boy, "In no uncertain terms, don't you forget what happened to these seven Korean patriots. The Japs killed them by hanging them in public square!"

The experience took root into the young boy's heart from then on.

Yu Yung Pil's anti-Japanese activity began when he was a student at the Japanese Kyung Ki Boy's Middle School. He passed the vigorous entrance exam and attended the school until March 1, 1919, when Korea declared independence from the Japanese occupation. For the event, the fourteen-year-old Yu Yung Pil had written, "Long Live Korea," on a large poster and then hung it on the wall of the school's main administration office building. Afterwards, he withdrew from the school and began attending Bo Sung Boys' Middle School, in Seoul.

When he got older and attended Waseda University in Tokyo, he continued his father's wishes to help the Korean government in exile in Chongqing, China. Helping the Korean government in exile was challenging and, at times, dangerous. Yu Yung Pil acted as a messenger between the Korean exiles and supporters back in Korea. Sometimes, Koreans would carry funds to the Korean government in China. For example, his father would scoop out the middle of soap bars and hide gold nuggets inside to avoid detection and have his son deliver it to the exiled government.

This was a dangerous mission. If he was caught by the Japanese police, he would be beaten and thrown into jail. In fact, one time, the Japanese police arrested Yu Yung Pil when he was trying to cross the border to China by train. The Japanese police dragged him by his shirt collar, through train car after train car. When the police were distracted with other matters, he took a chance, quietly unbuttoned his shirt, and then jumped off the still-moving train. He landed safely in a farm field.

All told, he was sent to Japanese prisons seven different times, as he wrote in his autobiography, *Hae Ddeu Nun Ji Pyung Sun* (*Sun Rising Horizon*), published in 1971 in Seoul.

After the country was liberated from the Japanese occupation, Yu's life was no less volatile and dangerous. During the time of the Republic of Korea, President Rhee Seung Mahn's regime also harassed him. Yu Chin San had opposed Rhee's dictatorial policies. Consequently, Rhee accused Yu of being a Communist sympathizer, as he did to many who disagreed with his policies. Consequently, Yu led a life of an opposition politician in the country where he had worked so hard for independence.

Now, after reuniting with his daughter and knowing where his son was, Yu Chin San considered himself lucky, compared with all the other men around him. At least his two children, Hyun Jung and Joong Yul, were both are alive.

It was a hot and humid August day when Hyun Jung and her father stepped into a makeshift Korean Army hospital located at the outskirts of Daegu.

The large hall was covered with wall-to-wall beds, filled with groaning, bandage-wrapped soldiers. A short nurse with a white cap pinned onto her short black hair led the pair to Joong Yul.

Joong Yul struggled to sit up in bed when he saw his father and sister walking toward him.

Yu Chin San looked at his son's arm, which was covered with dark reddish spots, and asked, "What's that on your arm? How did this all happen?"

Joong Yul paused a bit and then said, "I was leading my troops into battle and got hit. There I was, lying there in a ditch."

"So?" his father said, with his eyes wide.

"One of my soldiers, a private, spotted me." A brief silence followed, then Joong Yul continued, "He carried me on his back down to an infirmary."

Following his graduation from the Korean Military Academy, and after a brief duty at the Department of Defense in Seoul, Captain Yu Joong Yul had been shipped to the front line of the guerrilla-infested Ji Ri Mountain, in South Jula Do, the southwest province of Korea. The guerrillas acted fearlessly, trying to take over the nearby villages and kidnap or even kill anybody known to be pro-America or pro-South Korean government.

Adjusting the bloodstained bandage on his arm, Joong Yul said, "Father, we saw a lot." He paused and then continued, "A lot was going on there."

"Is that right?" his father said, encouraging him to say more.

"One time," Joong Yul said, "we found an abandoned campsite with a pot of rice still boiling."

"Really?" his father asked. "They had to take off for their lives, I guess."

"Father, I have seen my close allies and fellow army officers get blown up."

Yu Chin San listened quietly and then said, "What a sad tragedy that our people have come down to this: killing each other."

Yu Chin San and his daughter sat on wooden stools by the bed and listened attentively to Joong Yul's war story.

"Yes, Father, they are all out to take over," Joong Yul said.

"What's that over there?" his father asked, pointing to a tattered brown book lying on the table next to Joong Yul's bed.

"That's my lifesaver, Father," Joong Yul said. "A pocket dictionary." He placed his finger on a tattered spot of the small English/Korean, Korean/English dictionary. "A bullet hit it but didn't go through my chest. I had it in my breast pocket."

His father said, "You were always good at English. You were a good student; I am proud of you."

"I used it to look up words when I interpreted for the American soldiers," Joong Yul said and handed the worn dictionary to his father.

"I am glad that you were being helpful to those American soldiers," Yu Chin San said to his bandage-wrapped son. "We must thank the American parents for sending their young sons to help save us from the Communist invaders."

Joong Yul continued, "If it hadn't been for this little book, I would have been dead by now, Father."

"You shouldn't talk that way in front of your father," Yu Chin San scolded. It was regarded as being disrespectful to speak of dying in front of one's parents.

"It saved my life," Joong Yul said, lowering his eyes.

Born in 1921 to a family who valued education, his grandfather,

Yu Kung Duck Gong saw to it that Joong Yul had the best education and sent him away from Jin San to the province capital, Daejun, for his elementary school education. Afterwards, he was sent to Japan to continue with his studies. In 1945, the Japanese lost World War II, liberating Korea from the Japanese occupation; his parents urged him to return to Korea. He came back and taught English at a high school in Daejun. Later, he enrolled in the Korean Army Academy.

After listening attentively to his son, Yu Chin San covered his face with both hands. A few minutes later, he put his hands down and said, "I gave my son to my country. President Rhee Seung Mahn cannot accuse me of being a Communist sympathizer, as he often does to anyone he suspects of disloyalty."

When he saw his wounded son dozing off, Yu Chin San quietly gestured to Hyun Jung to leave.

With a heavy heart about the state of the country, and with his daughter at his side, Yu Chin San headed for the Kookje Hotel, his home away from home in the middle of Daegu.

Fifteen Men from Geum San

When Yu Chin San entered the Kookje Hotel, Secretary Jung told him, "A group of men have been waiting to see you, sir. They are from Geum San, sir."

Yu Chin San said, "Really? Who is it?"

"I recognize some of them," the Secretary answered. "These are the very guys responsible for our defeat at the last May election, sir." The secretary continued in a hushed voice. "They said they didn't have anyone else to turn to, sir."

"Oh?"

"Shall I turn them away, sir?" the secretary asked. "We don't owe them anything."

"Show them in," Yu Chin San said, without any hesitation. Yu then placed himself on a cushion at the main part of his tatami mat room. Motioning with his hand, he said to his daughter, "Come sit next to me."

Hyun Jung immediately obeyed.

Park, the leader of the fifteen men from Geum San, walked in with his entourage behind him. With their heads bent like caught escapees, the fifteen men kneeled in front of Yu Chin San.

Park lowered his head even more and began, "Please forgive us."

"Uh?" Yu Chin San said, widening his eyes.

Park continued, "We have no one but you, the honorable teacher, to turn to for help, sir."

"Oh?"

"Congresswoman Tae, sir," Park continued, shaking his head, "took off."

"Took off?"

"Yes, sir."

"So how can I help you?"

"We have no way to find a space without some connection to an important person, sir. We don't know anyone in this big city full of refugees, sir."

Yu Chin San listened without saying a word.

While the rest of the men still sat with their heads down, Park told how they snuck out of Geum San before dawn and had to sleep on the roadside and drink muddy water from a culvert underneath the highway to Daegu.

After listening attentively to Mr. Park, Yu Chin San said, "Tonight, you may all sleep here, in this room, with me."

"Yes?" Park responded with wide stretched eyes.

"We have no choice. We'll have to squeeze together in this room," Yu Chin San said, looking around his totally empty rectangular room with tatami mat floor. There was no furniture in the whole room. The only item in the room was a black upright piano at the far end of the room.

"Yes, sir."

"It's wartime," Yu Chin San said, adding, "The whole country is in a chaos."

As soon as he finished talking to Park, Yu Chin San had the piano moved to one corner of the room, making a triangle space for himself and Hyun Jung.

Yu Chin San knew exactly what to do next. First, he told his secretary to serve the fifteen men something to eat and drink. He then made a phone call to his very close friend, Congressman Suh Sang Ill, who had just been reelected to represent the city of Daegu to the South Korean Parliament.

The two men, Yu and Suh, were more than friends. They were very close comrades in the political opposition camp, committed to fight the Communists and oppose Rhee Seung Mahn's "inept policies," as they often referred to them.

In fact, during the recent election, only forty-five days before, Yu Chin San had taken a brief break from his own campaign in Geum San and came to Daegu to make a speech on behalf of the congressman. To be more specific, it was during the election of May 10, 1950, just before North Korea invaded the South.

For Suh's election, Yu Chin San had come down to Daegu and made a stinging speech against Rhee Seung Mahn's government: "If your family needs help with rice or medicine for illness," he had said to a large crowd of voters, "who would help you? Rhee Seung Man? No, your own Congressman Suh. Not the central government, not the old man, Rhee Seung Mahn, not Yi Ki Boong, the conniving Speaker of the Parliament." Yu Chin San had continued, "Yes, your own Congressman Suh."

The audience clapped loudly in agreement.

Congressman Suh was reelected to the South Korean Parliament in spite of Rhee Seung Mahn's all-out intimidation, including beating Suh supporters and jailing them on false charges.

Suh Sang Il was a plump-looking, jolly, short man in his late sixties. His graying sideburns gave the impression of warmth and maturity. He took particular delight in associating with Yu Chin San, who was fifteen years his junior. To Congressman Suh, Yu was smart and a gifted speaker. He knew Yu had a bright future in the opposition camp of Korean politics.

"I certainly will look into it," Congressman Suh said into the phone. Less than fifteen minutes later, Yu got a call back from the

Congressman: "Now, we have nothing but empty buildings and houses in this big city of ours. Folks just ran away for life and left everything."

Yu Chin San listened to what the congressman was saying.

"I have here a very nice twenty-bed hospital building, smack in the center of the city." Congressman Suh continued, "You could put your newly found family there, the fifteen men upstairs, and there is a very nice living quarters downstairs with a kitchen and even a garage. The hospital owner, Dr. Shin, is a good friend of mine. I'm sure he would be delighted to have the building used by good people like you and your new family."

As Congressman Suh suggested, the fifteen men from Geum San occupied upstairs, and Yu Chin San's own entourage of four, which included his daughter, Hyun Jung; Mr. Jung, his secretary/cook; Sohn, his driver; and Yu Chin San himself, lived on the first floor. Food was secondary in this war zone, where the enemy was so close and no one knew what would happen the next day. They were simply grateful they had a shelter, complete with roof and walls to protect them from straying bullets.

The men upstairs stayed quiet. They were grateful they didn't have to sleep outside on the road without any protection at all.

After settling into their hospital/home, the lives of the Yu family of four plus fifteen men appeared calm and normal as any family could be during wartime, as the victorious enemy, Communist, swiftly pushed the South Korean government down and down. As he had done even before the invasion by the Communist invaders, Hyun Jung's father attended the daily briefings at the office of Dr. Min Byung Soo, the Minister of Home Affairs.

Hyun Jung did her part by being a good girl and staying quiet, yet alert. The fifteen men were also quiet, as if no one lived up on the second floor. She was relieved, for she had had rougher times since the war broke out, suddenly finding herself without parents or family and having to constantly live under the threat of the

Communist invaders. Now, being with her father, she felt as though things couldn't be better for the thirteen-year-old. She was content.

As Hyun Jung grew accustomed to her life at this comfortable hospital-turned-home, she learned things weren't to remain the same very long.

They couldn't stay there any longer and had to run away again. The North Korean Communists, Democratic People's Republic of Korean (DPRK) army, as they called themselves, were lurking at Nakdong River, at the northern edge of the Daegu city limits.

35

The Enemies Are Closing In

This day, as he has been doing since coming to Daegu about two weeks before, Yu Chin San had gone to his daily briefing at the office of the Minister of Home Affairs with Dr. Min Byung Soo.

On this humid August morning, out of boredom, Hyun Jung opened the sliding door that led into the main square of the city of Daegu. To her surprise, she saw a stream of white-clad people running toward the south side of the town square, away from the city. Just then, her father came rushing through the back sliding door.

"Hurry up," Yu Chin San demanded. "Pack your things.... Not much to pack, is there?"

"Yes?" Hyun Jung asked. "What's happening, Father?"

"We must take off," he said. "Right now." His voice was tight with urgency. "The Communists have crossed Nakdong River at the northern border of Daegu."

Since leaving Seoul, packing up and running was something Hyun Jung had gotten pretty good at doing. She threw everything into her small brown bag with two handles. Then she went out and climbed into her family jeep, with the help of Mr. Jung.

As they were leaving Daegu, Hyun Jung saw Dr. Min, the

Minister of Home Affairs, riding on horseback and urging the people to go back, to remain in the city and not run away. The Minister believed, and it was widely understood, that the South Korean military would work harder to guard the city if the people stayed instead of running away.

However, Yu Chin San was determined to take his daughter to Myl Yang, about two hours south of Daegu, by car.

The only highway in the country, a narrow gravel-covered two-lane road that ran from north to south, was packed with refugees rushing southward. It was August 5; at the very same time, the United Nations army trucks were heading north, leaving mounds of dust clouds behind.

Yu Chin San asked Mr. Sohn to stop the jeep, and he got out of the vehicle with Hyun Jung to watch the trucks driving north on the opposite highway.

"They are the UN soldiers," Yu Chin San told his daughter with a twinkle in his eyes. "They came to help Korea." Hyun Jung listened attentively. Her father continued with a smile, "We are grateful."

"How do you know that, Father?"

"That's what we discussed this morning at Dr. Min's office, at the Minister of Home Affairs. These young men are from many different countries. They are from the United Nation's forces."

"What's United Nations, Father?"

"It's a group of nations that get together to help each other out when a country is unfairly attacked or threatened," Yu Chin San said, feeling proud of his daughter's questioning mind.

As they got back into the jeep, her father looked over and noticed a soldier hitchhiking.

Hyun Jung looked at the yellow-haired Western young man. He was about eighteen or nineteen years old.

"American, I think," her father said. "Give him a ride."

Mr. Sohn pulled over to give the young soldier a ride.

"Myl Yang?" the soldier asked.

"Yes, Myl Yang," her father said, in English. His studying English in college was useful.

They let the young soldier in and continued on with their drive southward, away from the Communist invaders.

"A deserter, I guess," her father said, quietly, in Korean.

It was dark when they arrived in Myl Yang. The young Western soldier went his way as soon as the jeep stopped. This small town was already packed with refugees. In fact, because it was much smaller than Daegu, Myl Yang was even more tightly packed than Daegu. There was no room to stand up without touching someone. If Daegu was to fall, Busan would be next. That would be the last city left in the Republic of Korea.

"I will check it out, sir," Mr. Jung, the secretary, said and walked into the town of Myl Yang. He came back rather shortly afterwards and said, "There is not a single spot in town for us to stay tonight, sir."

"Okay, then," Yu Chin San said to Mr. Jung, "You and Sohn sleep in the jeep tonight. My daughter and I will try to sleep on the riverbed."

"You will be so uncomfortable, sir."

"Look at all these people. They are all over the riverbed."

"Yes, sir."

"Tomorrow, we'll see what we can do."

"Yes, sir," Mr. Jung said, walking away toward the parked jeep near the main road.

That dark first night in Myl Yang, with twinkling stars above, the father and the daughter tried to sleep on the riverbank, with its lumpy rocks as their sleeping mat and the star-sparkling dark sky above as the ceiling. The last thing they cared about was how uncomfortable it was.

They stayed awake for most of the night. They listened attentively and monitored the sound of artillery from the battlefield. If the sound got louder, that meant that the enemy was winning, and they were getting closer. But if the sounds of gunshots and cannons were softer, that would mean the South was winning and the enemy was being pushed away. In the midst of monitoring the battle sounds, their minds gave in, and the father and the daughter dozed off.

Hyun Jung woke up to the sound of a stranger's voice, asking, "Can I borrow a puff of your cigarette, sir?"

As he did before in Daegu, her father found a house in Myl Yang for them. It was a traditional Korean house with gray tile roof and seven heavy gates with metal locks on each. The owner, Kim Bock Sung, was the richest person in town. He owned several local apple orchards that produced the nationally famous Myl Yang Apple Cider. The Kims had one child, a son, who had just turned twenty-one. The family wanted Yu Chin San to keep the son as his bodyguard. In return, they let Yu Chin San and his family use their guest quarters, which was complete with separate gate, well-stocked kitchen, and even a running stream with a school of goldfish swimming right in their front yard.

Hyun Jung, her father, Mr. Jung, and Mr. Sohn occupied the living quarters between the first and second gates.

Hyun Jung felt protected to be inside the thick wall with the heavy brass lock on the gate. She knew that as bad as it was, it was much better than where she had been for the last month, since the Communists invaded Seoul, June 25, to be exact.

Sadly, they couldn't stay in this nice house very long. The South Korean government was still being pushed yet farther down south. The victorious Communists continued to close in. The only city left in the whole country was the port city of Busan. It was the last city in the Republic of Korea.

"Where to, Father?"

"South, away from the Communists. My daughter, the South Korean government is losing the war and consequently losing the country."

36

No Place Else to Run To

In Busan, Yu Chin San, Mr. Sohn, Mr. Jung, and Hyun Jung checked into the large Harbor Hotel, located right in the center of the largest city in South Korea. The thirteen-year-old Hyun Jung felt safe as long as she was with her father. She even pretended things were as normal as they could be, and some of the little girl in her was slipping out.

She checked the pink bag she had been carrying since leaving Seoul and found out the high-top shoes and the family photos were gone. She had no idea when or how she lost them. However, she was glad that the peach-colored dress was still in her little bag. She decided to try on the dress before it, too, got lost. With the dress on, Hyun Jung felt like a pretty thirteen-year-old girl, for change. Her mother had bought it for her, and she had been carrying it all these days. She wanted to believe everything would work out for everyone, eventually. She felt warm inside.

To Hyun Jung's dismay, her father didn't say anything about how she looked with the pretty dress on. Instead, he was deep in thought and couldn't be distracted.

The hotel helper took their small breakfast table away and left the father and the daughter alone.

Yu Chin San paused for a moment. He was still in deep thought, and then, he said, "I am going to take you to Japan."

"Yes?" Hyun Jung answered, raising her eyes in disbelief. "Why?" she asked, frowning and looking directly at him. "Why, Father?"

"We have no place else to run to."

"Oh, Father!"

"Busan is the only place left," he explained, "If the Communists take Busan, that's it."

Hyun Jung understood what her father was saying. That's true. In reality, after the city of Busan, there was no other place for the South Korean people to run to.

"The Communists have taken all the cities," Yu Chin San stated. "Our government lost the entire country."

"Oh, father!"

"Your brother is in the hospital, wounded; no one knows what will happen to him."

Silence followed.

Hyun Jung looked up at him and said, "But I want to be with you, Father."

"I have a dear friend in Tokyo. That's where I will take you."

"No, Father."

"They will be happy to have you. We are friends from my college days at Waseda."

"How about you, Father?" Hyun Jung asked, looking directly at him. "What will you do?" She waited for his reply, but when she didn't get an answer, she asked, "Will you stay with me in Japan?"

"Oh, no," he answered and then paused, deep in thought.

"Why not, Father?"

"I will come back to Korea, to some mountain."

Hyun Jung frowned and then asked, "What did you just say?"

"I'll turn myself into a guerrilla and fight the Communists."

"Yes?" Hyun Jung looked at him and shook her head. "Father, I want to be with you, please!"

"No, it will be too rough for you; no!"

"Father, I will be a help to you. I don't want us to be separated again."

"I know, but …"

"I am tough. I walked all the way from Seoul, remember?"

"I know."

"Please!"

"I am grateful for that."

"I know how to survive the Communists."

Yu Chin San said, "Grandfather is in Jin San." He then said, "Your mother …" He looked away and then said, "The little boy, Han Yul …" Then, he turned back to his daughter and said, "You will be safe there, in Japan."

"I want to be with you, Father."

37

Epilogue

So Grateful to America

Thank God for America and President Harry S. Truman!

Hyun Jung didn't have to be brought to Japan for safety. And her father, Yu Chin San, didn't have to go up to some mountain and turn himself into a guerilla to fight the Communists.

At the insistence of President Truman, UN troops came, including soldiers from the US and twenty-two other nations.

The troops fought side by side with soldiers representing the United Nations and the soldiers from the Republic of Korea. On July 1953, the Korean War Armistice was signed by the representatives of the UN/US, China, and North Korea. The Republic of Korea did not sign this armistice, because Rhee Seung Mahn, the President of the Republic of Korea, wanted to have the whole of Korea unified (*Bukjin Tongil*), instead of being back to where it had been before the Korean War started.

In 1953, however, the Mutual Defense Treaty between the United States and South Korea was signed. Because of this treaty, US troops have been stationed in South Korea for all these years, even to present day. And under the Mutual Defense Treaty, the

South Korean military fought, side by side, with US soldiers against the Communists during the Vietnam War.

At this writing, the Korean peninsula is still divided at almost the same line as before the Communist invasion on June 25, 1950, when the Korean conflict began, the same North and South Korea. However, things have been much better for the Republic of Korea, also known as South Korea.

In 1950, when the Korean War began, South Korea was one of the poorest countries in the world, with $60 per capita annual income. That situation, however, wasn't too difficult to understand. After thirty-six years of ransacking occupation by the Japanese, Korea had been hollowed out of much of its resources. Additionally, Rhee Seung Mahn's government, which began in 1948 and lasted to 1960, did not have an economic development program to speak of.

After twelve presidents and much political turmoil years later, which included a military coup d'état in 1961, South Korea now is the sixth largest exporter and the eleventh largest economy in the world; it is also a member of G20. At the 2022 election, Yoon Suk-yeol of People Power Party was elected as South Korea's thirteenth president. Unlike his immediate predecessor, Moon Jae-in, Yoon's pro-America policy and firm stand toward Communist North Korea set the country in clearer line on the side of America and democracy.

On a personal level, although lives were spared, the invaders caused unforgettable trauma for a number of Hyun Jung's family members: The Communist guerillas in her hometown, Jin San, tried to kill Yu Kyung Duck Gong, her seventy-year-old grandfather, who refused to hide or run from them when they invaded the South. The Communists, in fact, had a knife on the grandfather's neck and planned to kill him by cutting his throat. The Communists, however, changed their mind and decided to "spare the old guy's life." The only reason was, as they repeated, "to catch the younger ones when they would visit this old man."

Yu Joong Yul, the South Korean army officer, survived the war, though his whole body was covered with shrapnel from the battles he fought against the Communist guerillas at the southern end of the Ji Ri Mountain.

Hyun Jung's mother, Kim Hyun Syn, and her eleven-year-old son, Han Yul, walked 115 miles, wearing a pair of thin rubber shoes, to the capital city of Jeonju, in Juhn La Book Do province, escaping sure persecution by the Communists. They called upon some relatives in Jeonju to take refuge. However, the people threw her bag back to her and told her to leave.

The mother and her little boy didn't have any other place to go in that big city. After walking aimlessly around Jeonju, the two came to a Buddhist temple. The *bhikkhuni* took them in to have her work as a kitchen maid. Hyun Jung's mother worked at the temple as a kitchen maid until she could safely return to her home in Jin San, when South Korea took back control of the country.

For thirteen-year-old Hyun Jung Yu, she and her classmates walked out of her dorm and left Seoul because "there was no more rice to feed you," as the girls were told by the principal of Ewha Girl's Middle School, where she was a student and lived in dormitory. For ten days, Hyun Jung walked south, trying to reach the South Korean government.

She was able to unite with her father with help of a KCIA Major she met at a battlefield checkpoint. After the armistice, she went back to Seoul and continued her education at Ewha Girl's Middle School and later attended Ewha Women's University. Later, Hyun Jung came to America to continue on her education. She has taught at American public schools in Arizona and in North Carolina.

After the 1953 armistice, Hyun Jung's father, Yu Chin San, led an active political life in the Republic of Korea. After being the Chairman of the Anti-Communist League for Korean Youth, he served in the

South Korean Parliament for seven terms. When he passed away in 1974, he was the Chairman of Shin Min Dang, the Major opposition party. He published an autobiographical book, *Hae Ddeu Nun Ji Pyung Sun* (*Sun Rising Horizon*). He loved democracy and America.

In 1969, Yu Chin San visited America at the invitation of the US State Department. During this visit, he told his daughter, with hopeful expression, "Our Korean people, also can make *Ramen* noodles, like the Japanese do."

Yu Chin San would have been very happy to learn about the technological and economic success story of today's Republic of Korea, the country he loved and fought for almost all of his life.

Korean Words

azumma (aunt, usually young, not older than fifty)

bahdook (Korean chess game)

bahn mahl (informal speech)

bahp (steamed grain)

banchan (side dishes)

bbahl-gehng-ee (Communist, red)

Dong Hae (Eastern Sea)

dongseng (fellowship younger sister or younger brother)

hal-ahbuhjee (grandfather)

hal-muni (grandmother)

hangul (Korean writing)

kkoma (little kid)

kyoje unee (fellowship big sister)

sunbae unees (upper-class sisters)

ueng (okay, to friend or to younger person)

unnie (older sister)

yangban (nobility, upper class)

Names

Bae Jung Ja (eleventh grader, Ewha Girl's Middle School)

Dr. Min Byung Soo (Minister of Home Affairs, Republic of Korea, Name Changed)

Jung Joo Sill (twelfth grader, Group Leader, Ewha Girl's Middle School)

Kim Keum Ja (eleventh grader, Ewha Girl's Middle School)

Kim Tae Young (Group Leader. Name changed)

Ko Yung Hee (twelfth grader, Yu Hyun Jung's Fellowship Older Sister)

Major Choi (Director of Korean Central Intelligence Agency (KCIA))

Park Ki Taek (Group Leader. Name changed)

Rhee Syngman (President of South Korea: 1948–1960)

Tae Jung Shin (defeated Yu Chin San in 1950 National Election for Congress; name changed)

Yu Chin San (Yu Hyun Jung's father)

Yu Joong Yul (Yu Chin San's wounded son)

Yu Eun Ja (Hyun Jung's friend at Ewha. Same last name but unrelated)

Yu Hyun Jung (student at Ewha, the author of *Thousand Lucks*)

NOTE:
To respect privacy, certain names have been changed.
In Korean culture, the family name comes first.

About the Author

Diana Yu's first work of nonfiction, *Winds of Change: Korean Women in America*, received a National Press Club award in two categories: Importance of Subject and High Quality of Writing. Diana's first novel, *Sylvia's Garden*, received a Five Star award by Online Book Reviewers.

Diana was a post-doctoral Fellow in East Asian Studies at Harvard. She earned a doctorate in Higher Education Administration and International Education from The George Washington University. After receiving an MA and BA from Arizona State University, Diana taught in public schools in Arizona and in North Carolina.

In Korea, she studied at the Ewha Women's University after graduating from Ewha Girl's Middle and High School.

Printed in the USA
CPSIA information can be obtained
at www.ICGtesting.com
LVHW041824091123
763047LV00124B/347/J